HOW TO
RAISE
A
Lady

OTHER GENTLEMANNERS™ BOOKS

How to Be a Gentleman
John Bridges

A Gentleman Entertains
John Bridges and Bryan Curtis

As a Gentleman Would Say
John Bridges and Bryan Curtis

A Gentleman Gets Dressed Up
John Bridges and Bryan Curtis

A Gentleman Walks Down the Aisle
John Bridges and Bryan Curtis

Toasts and Tributes
John Bridges and Bryan Curtis

50 Things Every Young Gentleman Should Know
Kay West with John Bridges and Bryan Curtis

50 Things Every Young Lady Should Know
Kay West with John Bridges and Bryan Curtis

How to Be a Lady
Candace Simpson-Giles

As a Lady Would Say
Sheryl Shade

How to Raise a Gentleman
Kay West

A Lady at the Table
Sheryl Shade with John Bridges

A Gentleman at the Table
John Bridges and Bryan Curtis

A Gentleman Abroad
John Bridges and Bryan Curtis

HOW TO RAISE

RAISE

A

Lady

REVISED AND EXPANDED

....

A CIVILIZED GUIDE TO HELPING YOUR DAUGHTER THROUGH HER UNCIVILIZED CHILDHOOD

KAY WEST

THOMAS NELSON
Since 1798

NASHVILLE   DALLAS   MEXICO CITY   RIO DE JANEIRO

Published in Nashville, Tennessee, by Thomas Nelson. Thomas Nelson is a registered trademark of Thomas Nelson, Inc.

Thomas Nelson, Inc., titles may be purchased in bulk for educational, business, fund-raising, or sales promotional use. For information, please e-mail SpecialMarkets@ThomasNelson.com.

ISBN: 978-1-4016-0463-9 (repack)

The Library of Congress has cataloged an earlier edition as follows:

West, Kay, 1995–
  How to raise a lady / by Kay West.
     p. cm.
  ISBN: 978-1-55853-941-9 (hardcover)
  ISBN: 978-1-40160-186-7 (leather edition)
  1. Child rearing. 2. Etiquette for children and teenagers. 3. Etiquette for girls. I. Title.
  HQ769.W447 2001
  649'.133—dc21
2001004339

Printed in the United States of America

12 13 14 15 16 WOR 6 5 4 3 2 1

For my parents, who taught me manners; For my children, who taught me parenting; And to RRT for the rest

CONTENTS

INTRODUCTION

*B*abies are miracles, miniature models of full-grown humans, carrying the genes and DNA that form the framework of a stunning beauty or a natural athlete, an ear for music, an eye for art, a brain for business. It's all in that precious little package, the seeds of a full-grown girl with sparkly green eyes, curly red hair, a dimpled smile, long legs, an allergy to strawberries, a love of poetry, and an inexplicable attraction to reptiles.

One thing a baby is not born with and a young lady will not learn unless she is taught are good manners. Among the hundreds of expenses that constitute the soaring costs of raising a child from conception to graduation, the development of manners is the least costly. In fact, it is absolutely free. And the bonus is that teaching your little girl good manners is the one investment you can make with guaranteed returns. She may be trilingual by the time she's in second grade, but if she doesn't say "please" and "thank you" in at least one language, she is at a disadvantage among those who do. She may be able to compose an impressively thoughtful haiku, but if she doesn't write her grandmother to say thank you for a very thoughtful birthday gift, she may not receive a gift on her next birthday. She may be the leading scorer on her eight-year-old's soccer team, but if she berates a teammate who misses a key shot, she's a poor candidate to be a leader.

While rules of proper etiquette define a formal code of behavior and can be quite complicated, good manners are born from common courtesy and common courtesy is quite simple. Courtesy is based on respect, civility, kindness, and consideration. It is being mindful of others, whether you are in their presence or not. Courtesy walks hand in hand with good manners, and both are the embodiment of the Golden Rule: Do unto others as you would have them do unto you.

Good manners are the practical applications of kindness. They will open more doors, charm more acquaintances, and make more memorable first impressions than all the French, flute, and tennis lessons combined.

Good manners begin with the assimilation of examples set by parents. *How to Raise a Lady* is a book for parents of girls. It is for parents who want to do the right thing, but who may need a few pointers themselves. This is not a book of formal etiquette, but a guide to good manners supported by a commonsense collection of real-life advice, time-tested tips, and lessons learned. This instruction manual will prove to be as helpful for fully grown humans as it is for those still in the developmental stages. The basics can be acquired by toddlers and with daily application will last a lifetime. It is never too soon to begin or too late to catch up.

LEADING THE WAY TO GOOD MANNERS

26 Things to Remember

Use "please," "thank you," and "excuse me."
Always.

Wait your turn.

Be generous with compliments and stingy with
criticism.

Listen to your child when she speaks to you, even
if you've heard it before.

Do not discipline your child in front of others.

Do not correct any child on her manners, other
than your own, and always do that privately.

Be clear about what you expect.

Be consistent.

Do not give in to temper tantrums.

Do not lose your temper.

Admit when you are wrong; offer an apology when you owe one.

Let your child know when a discussion has become a decision.

Words *can* hurt; do not hurl them about as weapons.

Respect your child's privacy and boundaries. Knock first.

Do not impose your ideology, and respect those whose ideology differs from your own.

Agree to disagree.

Give credit where credit is due.

Hold the door.

Lend a hand.

Be a good sport.

Be a gracious loser, and a generous winner.

Give more than you are asked.

Don't take more than you need.

Leave a place cleaner than you found it.

Do not respond to rudeness with rudeness.

Winning is not the only thing, and nice girls do finish first.

Chapter One

PLEASE, THANK YOU, EXCUSE ME, AND OTHER EARLY SOCIAL INTERVENTIONS

The first year of your daughter's life is chock-full of milestones: the first time she sleeps through the night, the first time she rolls over, sits up, crawls, pulls herself up, and the first step. Each of those achievements is easily documented. The first word, however, is a bit more intangible. Parents straining to hear their little girl's primitive attempts at spoken communication will eagerly interpret the most garbled babbling as "Mama" and "Dada." It is nothing less than joyful music to their ears. Slightly less harmonious will be the next addition to her teensy lexicon: "no." In its earliest and most experimental stages, it typically does not indicate rudeness, but a simpler way to communicate displeasure than crying and screaming. It is also an easier word for tiny mouths to form than the more agreeable and pleasant "yes." Though it will be some time before she includes verbs, adverbs, adjectives, and protocol in her conversations, that doesn't mean she isn't soaking up the patterns of speech used by the adults and older siblings in her home.

The best way to introduce and promote mannerly conduct is by example. Children want to emulate the adults in their lives and fit in with the rest of the family. If the words "please" and "thank you" are used without exception in your home, your budding young lady will follow suit. Using "please" and "thank you" yourself is also an opportunity to reward and promote other courteous behavior.

Except in the case of an emergency, encourage the use of the word "please" by not responding to a request until the word is employed. Don't expect a three-year-old to deliver lengthy sentences such as "May I please have a glass of juice?" but help her see the difference between a request and a demand. "Juice!" is a demand that grates on the nerves and will go unheeded; "Juice, please?" is a request, so pleasing to the adult ear it is likely to be met with the cheerful bestowal of the coveted item.

When your daughter's request is granted, she then responds, "Thank you." Adults should, in turn, respond to this simple display of gratitude with a modest expression of approval, "You're welcome," with a smile or quick hug. Rewards are not necessary for behavior that is eventually expected to be a matter of course, with the possible exception of potty training. In that taxing endeavor, the reward system is encouraged. Reserve your applause for accomplishments that deserve it, like an excellent report card or a soccer goal.

It is one small but impressive step from "please" and "thank you" to "yes, please" and "no, thank you," but one not to be expected until the child has mastered the former and uses them as habit. At that point, "Would you like a glass of juice?" has two appropriate responses: "Yes, please" or "No, thank you."

The next phrase to be added to a young lady's socially correct vocabulary is "excuse me." The opportunities for its use will present themselves again and again:

If a young lady inadvertently burps aloud, she says, "Excuse me."

If a young lady accidentally bumps into someone or steps on toes, the appropriate way to make amends is simply by saying "Excuse me."

A young lady does not interrupt adults when they are engaged in conversation. If the conversation is a lengthy one, and she has a pressing need that must be promptly attended to, then she might say, "Excuse me, Mommy. I really need to go to the bathroom now!" An attentive mommy will cease her discussion of the novel her book club is reading, and attend to her daughter's request.

Should a young lady need to have something repeated to her because it was unclear, or she was unable to hear, she says "Excuse me?" She does not say "What?" or even worse, "Huh?"

Your Daughter Is Becoming a Young Lady If . . .

She uses "please," "thank you," and "excuse me" on a consistent basis.

She does not point out other children's lack of manners.

When she doesn't understand something that was said to her, she says, "Excuse me?" or "I'm sorry, I didn't hear what you said."

Parent Pointers

Use "please," "thank you," and "excuse me" in all encounters.

Say "please" when making a request of your daughter.

Say "thank you" to your daughter after she fulfills that request.

Say "excuse me" if you must interrupt her, even if you are becoming impatient with her scene-by-scene description of the movie she just saw.

Occasionally note your daughter's developing sense of good manners.

Compliment your daughter's friends on their good manners.

Try This at Home

To discourage telephone interruptions from my daughter, I hold my hand up in front of her face like a policeman stopping traffic, or turn my back altogether. Unless it is an emergency, I do not stop my conversation until its natural conclusion. As she has gotten older, she has learned not to verbally interrupt; instead, she writes notes: "May I please have a Popsicle?" or "May Audrey spend the night?" and holds them up for me to read. It's an amusing and acceptable compromise.

Some Good Advice

My daughter has been so drilled in the use of "please,"
"thank you," and "excuse me" that she sometimes
automatically prompts others on its use. If I give
a glass of milk to one of her friends, who takes it
without saying "thank you," Joy has been known to
point out the friend's lack of manners. However, it
is the parents' job to teach their own children good
manners and that the core of good manners is not
steadfast attendance to the rules of etiquette, but it is
kindness, respect, and consideration for others.

Chapter Two

YES SIR, NO SIR, AND OTHER REGIONAL DIVIDES

I spent the first half of my life in the North and am closing in on that much time in the South. The Mason-Dixon line is named for the eighteenth-century English astronomers who surveyed this line of demarcation from 1763 to 1767 to resolve a border dispute between British colonies in colonial America, as well as a dividing line between the slave- and non-slave-owning states. Well after the War between the States ended, it came to symbolize the distinct cultural divide between the upper and lower halves of our country.

Thanks to the transitory nature of modern life, not to mention the assimilation of so many different ethnic influences into the fabric of our country, a national homogenization has occurred. But certain broad generalizations persist: people who live below the Mason-Dixon line often consider a Yankee's typical straightforwardness to be discourteous. Conversely, many Northerners take a Southerner's love for idle chitchat with complete strangers as an unwelcome and extremely annoying intrusion.

Southerners also have a tendency to cloak what they really mean in euphemisms. For instance, two Southern ladies are having lunch and discussing an acquaintance who recently lost her children's entire college education fund playing the stock market. They speculate on what could have led her to do such a careless thing. "You know, until he died, he always took care of their money. She's just darling, and the most wonderful mother, but she never did have a head for figures. Bless her heart." In the North, that same conversation would have gone like this: "Thank God Tom always took care of their money because she can't balance a checkbook to save her life."

When the church I attend in Nashville called a clergyman from New York City to be our rector, many were a little apprehensive about a Yankee in the pulpit. But the new reverend was warm and charming and gave brilliant sermons in a frank and straightforward manner. After services one morning he was talking with a group of church members who asked him what he had found to be the biggest difference between Yankees and Southerners. "Well, in the North, you know exactly where you stand with people. In the South, no one ever seems to say what they mean." Bless his heart, he just hadn't learned the language yet.

Growing up in the Northeast, the only time I heard the words "ma'am" and "sir" was when watching television. I thought it was a charming, old-fashioned custom, but when I moved south, I was amazed to find that this habit was not a television fabrication but a way of life for many families.

The use of "sir" and "ma'am" seems to be a practice that parents encourage more in boys than girls, but if you have both genders in your home, it would be inconsistent and confusing to ask Charles to use "sir" and "ma'am," and not Susan. Teaching your son or daughter such politesse is a matter of personal taste. For some adults, the policy governing the use of "ma'am" and "sir" is not grounded in tradition or formalities but is a means of eliminating such grating responses as "Yeah," "Nah," or unintelligible grunts.

If you choose to require their usage, be consistent. Require the titles for both close and distant family members and for both friends and professional acquaintances. As your daughter gets older, she may measure the use of such titles by age and status, with age being the primary factor. As adults are always older than children, then "sir" and "ma'am" are used, and even if your ten-year-old is the star of her own hit television series, adults are still, by virtue of their years, her superiors. As an adult, status becomes the primary measure of when to use these titles, such as when addressing those in authority, like a boss or a police officer.

If your daughter attends a school where formal deportment is part of the curriculum, her teachers may require the use of "sir" and "ma'am" in the classroom. If that is inconsistent with your habits at home, the wishes of the teacher always take precedence in the classroom.

Your Daughter Is Becoming a Young Lady If . . .

She routinely uses "sir" and "ma'am" if it is a practice in your family.

She doesn't make fun of people's accents or their regional or cultural speech patterns.

She does not make disparaging remarks about the customs or practices of another culture; for example, "That is so weird!" or "I can't believe you eat that!"

She follows the rules and practices of conduct when visiting someone else's home, such as removing shoes at the front door.

She bows her head and is respectful of a blessing before a meal, regardless of whether she practices the same in her home.

Parent Pointers

Use "sir" and "ma'am" in appropriate situations if you require its use from your daughter.

Do not require the use of "sir" and "ma'am" from anyone other than your own daughter.

Do not discourage its use by girls who do, even if your own daughter does not. It is not appropriate to monitor another person's manners.

Deliver a reminder, when needed, in a quiet and
subtle manner. Veteran users of "sir" and
"ma'am" report that once mastered, it becomes
a lifelong habit.

Try This at Home

I do not require my daughter to use "sir" and "ma'am,"
but I do insist—over and over—that she be as articulate
as possible, particularly when speaking to the elderly.
If she mutters or drawls or runs her words together, I
make her repeat it until it is crystal clear. My particular
pet peeve is when she doesn't hear or understand
something and responds, "Huh?" That is incorrect; the
proper way to ask someone to repeat what they have
said is, "Excuse me?" or, "I'm sorry, I didn't understand
what you said." Insist that your daughter speak clearly,
even if you seem to be nitpicky.

Some Good Advice

Moving is always stressful, but moving from one region of the country to another can be extremely daunting. Do a lot more listening than talking and more watching than doing. Don't be afraid to ask your new neighbors to tell you about themselves and their state. New Yorkers moving to Texas will soon find that barbecue is not something you do, but something you eat; that driving friendly means pulling over to the shoulder of the road to let a faster-moving vehicle pass; and that when a store owner says "Come back" as you leave the register, it is not a personal invitation but a figure of speech.

Chapter Three

INTRODUCTIONS, GREETINGS, AND LEAVINGS

onths before my daughter made her grand entrance at 5:49 a.m. on April 23, 1990, she was being introduced to family, friends, colleagues, and even complete strangers via her grainy black-and-white ultrasound image that I carried with me wherever I went. Given the slightest bit of encouragement, I would pull out the photo and show off the precious little five-month-old fetus that more closely resembled a tootsie roll with appendages than a little girl.

Less than four hours after she was born, my hospital room was full of people cooing over my precious baby girl, peering into her little bassinet, admiring all 7 pounds, 15 ounces, and 20 inches of her. "Hello, I'm your Grandma Joyce!" "Hello, I'm your grandma Edwina!" "Hello, I'm your Aunt Rachel!"

Introductions are a snap at that age, when your little girl can do not much more than stare back at the smiling face hovering inches from her own. As she gets a little older, she may even greet her new friend with a delightful, toothless smile and grasp a grown-up finger in her itty-bitty hand.

First impressions count, and it's almost impossible for a baby to make a bad first impression. Even as they reach the toddler years, young children are usually given the benefit of the doubt. Simply by not appearing sullen, a young girl who does nothing more than smile and venture a shy "hello" will be considered well mannered.

For children, particularly young or shy children, introductions can be extremely uncomfortable. In introducing your daughter to the practice of receiving and eventually making introductions, keep her age and level of intro- or extroversion in mind.

Once a girl is spending more time in the world— at school, on a soccer team, in a ballet class—more can be expected of her. By the time she is approaching those tricky tween years, and her social circle has widened, she should have mastered the basics of responding to introductions. She can even begin performing them when necessary.

Introductions can be tricky to navigate, even for a grown-up, but a fumbling introduction is better than none at all. When in a group of people, it is extremely rude to encounter an acquaintance or colleague and not perform some type of introduction. If you have completely forgotten a name, you might forewarn the people you are with, in the hopes that they can help you by introducing themselves first. If that doesn't work, it's better to confess your poor memory than to fail to make an introduction. If your daughter sees you practicing this basic form of social inclusion without exception, no matter how awkwardly executed it may be, she will come to see that introductions are an integral component of courteous behavior.

According to traditional etiquette, there are three basic rules of introduction:

1. A man is always introduced to a lady.
2. A young person is always introduced to an older person.
3. A less important person is always introduced to a more important person.

The first two are fairly simple; the third can be more complicated, particularly in modern times when status is dictated by so many particulars. Certainly, your idea of an important person will be wildly divergent from your daughter's. I advise weighing in with the first two guidelines, unless one in your party of strangers is the president or Oprah Winfrey.

When introducing young children to an adult, age takes precedence over gender, so the child should always be introduced to the adult. "Anna, I'd like you to meet Reverend Stevens." "Reverend Stevens, this is my daughter Anna." Unless she has had extensive beauty pageant experience, a four-year-old girl may be confused and perhaps even frightened by an adult thrusting out a hand to be shaken, and considerate people do not put children in that position. A young girl can simply try to make brief eye contact and say "hello."

Another rule of thumb is that an older person always extends his or her hand first to a younger one, so in the event that you do have a future Miss Congeniality on your hands, do advise your outgoing little girl to wait and follow the adult's lead.

As a girl matures it is important to teach her the value of standing up straight, making eye contact, and speaking clearly. Slouching about, looking down at the floor or at an area somewhere over the introductee's shoulder implies that she is bored or has something to hide.

When a young girl is introduced to a grown-up she may respond with something simple: "Hello" is better than "Hi." If the person to whom she is being introduced continues the conversation with "How are you?" she may say, "Fine, thank you." A helpful lesson to be learned early on is that strangers do not really want to know that your goldfish died or you scraped your knee, but that "How are you?" is just another form of polite speech.

Girls older than seven or eight are capable of a brief conversation. If a grown-up asks your daughter about school or camp, you may be tempted to answer for your child, particularly if she is slow or hesitant in responding. Resist this temptation, along with the urge to nudge or poke her. Allow her to work through this exchange and commend her later for her pleasant response. When the exchange is completed and you are leaving, a younger girl can simply say "good-bye." A girl older than ten may be encouraged to add, "It was nice to meet you."

Your Daughter Is Becoming a Young Lady If . . .

She refers to an adult as Mr., Mrs., or Ms. until she is asked to do otherwise.

She greets and converses with adult friends and acquaintances in a friendly and courteous manner.

She shows respect by standing when introduced.

She performs introductions, using first and last names among peers and Mr. and Mrs. when referring to adults.

When introducing members of her family to others, she explains the relationship. "This is my mother, Mrs. Chappell, and my sister Lily."

She does not roll her eyes or scowl when an adult relative is determined to pinch her cheek, pat her head, hug, or kiss her but simply bears up as best she can. She will be confronted with far more unappealing social situations later in her life.

Parent Pointers

Know the basic rules of introductions.

Always make introductions when people in a group do not know one another.

Always include your daughter in the introductions, but do not require more from her than she is comfortable with.

Do not tell your daughter to kiss or hug someone when it has not been requested of her.

Try This at Home

Act out some scenarios at home, enlisting the aid of siblings, spouse, or friends. Pretend you and your daughter are in a public place and you run across a teacher from her school. Allow your daughter to make the introductions: "Dad, this is Mrs. Potter, the art teacher at my school. Mrs. Potter, this is my father, Lindsey Chappell." Pretend you run into one of your clients at a mall. "Anna, this is Julie Thompson. She does our design work. Julie, this is my oldest daughter, Anna." Anna responds, "Hello, Mrs. Thompson," and offers her hand if Mrs. Thompson offers hers first. Practice a firm handshake.

Some Good Advice

People often say they cannot remember names,
but that is less faulty memory and more a lack of
focus during an introduction. When people are
introduced to you, repeat their name back to them
at that moment, and again when you say good-bye.
This practice will help you focus more during the
introduction, and repeating the name will help you
remember.

Chapter Four

SHOPPING, OFFICES, AND WAITING ROOMS

*B*efore she was a year old, my daughter had been to more places and logged more miles than I had in the first eighteen years of my life. My mother was a stay-at-home mom with five children, and we rarely went anywhere en masse outside of an occasional outing to a park or swim club. She reserved her errands, grocery shopping, and appointments for times when she could persuade a neighbor to keep an eye on us or on a night my father was not working.

As a freelance writer, I do much of my work at home, but in the days before e-mail, my baby girl came with me to deliver stories, meet with editors, and even on some assignments. Happy and easygoing, she was no more difficult to tote about than the diaper bag. Once she was mobile and talking, I could no longer take her on work assignments, but she and her brother went everywhere else with me.

Beginning at about the age of four, a young lady should be taught the basics of good manners in public places. Unlike teenagers who would prefer to think they were hatched from an egg, young children want to spend time with their parents, whether sitting down to hear a story, playing *Chutes and Ladders*, or going along to the bank. Errands might not be as much fun as playing a game, but children must eventually learn that even unpleasant things can be borne with as pleasant a nature as possible.

For quick errands such as banking or running to the dry cleaner or drugstore, girls do not need to bring along toys, but they should be told how long the errands will take. Children should not be required to accompany their parents on lengthy shopping expeditions.

No other type of business or service tolerates such disregard for another person's time than do the government and doctors. Since this seems to be the norm, however, pediatricians' offices usually come equipped with toys and books. In a group practice, though, don't count on there being enough to go around. You should bring something along just in case, like a self-contained puzzle or a coloring book.

If you must bring your daughter to the office, even for a short while, it is your responsibility to provide her with something to hold her attention. Under no circumstances is she to touch things that do not belong to her or to rummage through someone's desk.

When shopping, a young lady stays close to her parent. If the young lady cannot control herself in the grocery store, she will have to ride in the cart until she can. This applies to ten-year-olds as well as four-year-olds. In stores and offices, a young lady keeps her hands to herself. When my daughter is forced to accompany me on a shopping expedition, I try to leave a little time—even just a few minutes—to go someplace she enjoys as recognition of her patience and good behavior.

Your Daughter Is Becoming a Young Lady If . . .

She stays close to her parents when shopping or in other public places.

She is not greedy with samples in a grocery store.

She does not badger her parent or other adults to buy things for her.

She does not rummage around, exploring desks or closets in offices or peeking under doors in dressing rooms.

In banks, post offices, and other places where transactions are conducted, she does not scribble all over deposit slips and change of address forms.

In offices, she does not make photocopies of her face on the company copier or raid the office kitchen without permission.

She gives her seat to an adult in a crowded waiting room.

In waiting rooms, she does not hog all the books or puzzles to herself, but takes just one as she needs it, then returns it to the pile when she is finished.

She uses trash receptacles in public places. A young lady does not leave a candy wrapper or used tissue on a chair in a waiting room or a counter in a bank.

Parent Pointers

Do not expect your daughter to endure a lengthy shopping trip unless it is to a toy or candy store.

When going to the doctor's office or someplace where you will be expected to wait, provide something to occupy your daughter's attention.

When your daughter asks to go on errands with you, let her know how long you plan to be gone.

Do not succumb to your daughter if she badgers you to buy her a treat; otherwise you can expect a lifetime of badgering.

Do not promise a reward at the outset, but if there is time, offer some token of appreciation if her behavior was good.

Try This at Home

Whenever we go to a large store or a mall, I remind my children to stay in the store if we get separated. I would never leave the store without them, so if we both adhere to this rule, even if we can't see each other, we can know that we are both in the store somewhere. Practice what your child should do if she realizes that she has somehow ended up separated from her parent. She should find an employee or security guard and tell that person that she is lost. When my daughter was old enough—ten was the age I set—to be in a toy store by herself (for no more than fifteen minutes) while I went next door to the pharmacy to pick up a prescription, I reminded her *not* to leave the store and *not* to go anywhere with anyone else. Make sure your child knows how to react to a stranger making advances.

SOME GOOD ADVICE

If you encounter an obviously lost child in a mall or department store, do not touch the child, but bend or kneel so that you are on eye level, speak quietly and kindly, tell the child your full name, and ask if he or she is lost. Do not ask the child to come with you as he or she may have been taught not to go anywhere with strangers. Send someone else to get a store employee or security guard, and stay with the child until they return. They can then employ store policy to find the missing, and probably frantic, parent.

Chapter Five

PLAYGROUNDS, PLAYDATES, AND PLAYING WELL WITH OTHERS

"Play," said Montaigne, "is a child's most serious action." It is how they learn, how they explore, how they develop motor skills, and when engaged with playmates, it offers valuable lessons in compromise, courtesy, and respect and kindness to others. Plop two or more babies or even toddlers in a room together, and there will be very little interaction, with the exception of an occasional lunge for someone else's toy and a howl of protest, perhaps even a bite in response.

As they get older and more social, it is important for children to learn how to interact with one another. Working moms and stay-at-home moms are all familiar with the concept of "playdates," a snappy, pop-culture term for playing with other children. Rather than just shooing her child out the back door with a vague directive to "go play" as my mother used to do, one mom calls another on the phone and invites Sarah over to play with Lauren at 10:00 a.m. next Tuesday. Sarah's mom drives her over to Lauren's house; four hours later, Lauren's mom drives Sarah home. Pre-, during-, and post-playdate, there are certain codes of behavior for hostesses and guests.

When a young lady goes to another child's home for a playdate, she does not tote along a case full of her own toys. If the girls are in the Barbie stage (something that lasted all of fifteen minutes with my daughter), she can bring along a few of her own dolls, minus the accessories. The last thing a house with a little girl needs is more itty-bitty plastic Barbie shoes clogging up the vacuum cleaner.

If plans have been made to ride tricycles, bicycles, or rollerblades, then the visiting girl brings her own equipment. A hostess does not ride her bike if her friend did not bring her own and she cannot provide one for her friend.

The hostess shares her toys; very small children may need to have the concept explained before the guest arrives. Many girls collect dolls or figurines that are not meant to be played with. If she owns something of great value, put it away before the guest arrives. When at another child's home, a young lady treats the toys as if they were her own. If she accidentally breaks her friend's toy, she apologizes, and the hostess should accept her apology graciously. The hostess defers to the guest's wishes with regard to play. When a compromise cannot be reached, it may be necessary for a parent to intervene.

A good guest follows the rules of the host home when she is visiting (e.g., no eating in the living room, no jumping on the furniture, no running down the hall, no sliding down the banister). Even if the visiting child breaks one of those rules in an egregious fashion, a parent never raises her voice to another child.

A good hostess doesn't get a drink or a snack without offering the option to her guest as well. She does not correct her friend's manners, but may point out that her mother does not allow food or drinks in the living room. When she has company, the hostess does not engage in exclusionary play such as computer solitaire. A guest should help her hostess clean up, but if the guest does not, a hostess does not insist.

Many mothers of young children form mothers' groups or playgroups. From the time my children were babies until they began school, I was in a group of about eight mothers and, eventually, sixteen children. We met every Thursday morning from early spring to late fall at a child-friendly park equipped with paved trails for tricycles and scooters, a small playground, a large sandy area for digging, plenty of grass, and picnic tables. Everyone packed a lunch and blankets, and for the next three hours—or until complete child meltdown occurred—the mothers engaged in adult conversation on subjects ranging from potty training to politics. Under our collective eye, our children were taught the rules of fair play on a playground. Field trials proved to us that young boys are more aggressive than young girls, but that young girls are more exclusionary than young boys. The following rules apply to both sexes, but some must be more assertively enforced:

No shoving or hitting.

Do not throw anything at another child.

Share the toys with other children.

Do not spit water on other children.

Wait your turn in line for the slide or climbing stations.

Do not push or crowd other children in line in an attempt to speed them up.

Do not hog the swings, but take turns. If a young lady cannot assess an appropriate length of time for a turn, an adult should set and enforce limits.

Do not knock down another child's sand castle or mud fort.

Young ladies do not form small cliques with the purpose of excluding other children. The exception is Girls Only Clubs. Boys are then free to form a Boys Only Club.

Your Daughter Is Becoming a Young Lady If . . .

She checks with her parents before setting a playdate.

She does not invite herself for a playdate.

She does not ridicule another child about the quality of her toys.

She asks politely for a glass of water if she is thirsty but waits for the hostess to offer any food.

She asks where the bathroom is instead of searching for it.

When using the bathroom, she closes the door, flushes the toilet when finished, washes her hands, and returns the towel to the rack.

If she doesn't feel well, she tells a parent immediately.

She does not leave the host home or yard without telling a grown-up.

She helps smaller children on the playground.

She helps carry her things to the car when the time comes to leave the playground or park. When it is time to leave, a young lady comes when called.

Parent Pointers

Be sure to talk to a parent when making arrangements for a playdate. Set a definite time for the playdate to begin and end and provide a number where you can be reached.

Always introduce yourself to the parents of your daughter's playdate.

For young girls, always provide a change of clothes in case of an accident.

Always inform the hostess's parent of your daughter's allergies or any idiosyncratic fears.

Never send a sick child to another child's home.

Do not allow a sick child to participate in playgroup.

Inform your daughter's friend's parents about the boundaries you've set concerning television, movies, the computer, and snacks.

Gently enforce your rules in your car and home (e.g., "We do not use the words 'shut up' and 'stupid' in our house").

Do not correct another child's manners: "What do you say?" will embarrass a child who hasn't been taught to say "please" or "thank you."

Put a stop to another child's unacceptable behavior, but do not punish her for it. That is the job of her parents, and depending on the

extreme nature of the behavior, you should
mention it without recrimination to the child's
parent.

Remove your daughter from the playgroup for
inappropriate or unacceptable conduct,
and enforce rules of civil behavior. If the
unacceptable behavior continues, skip one of
the playgroup sessions until your child can
control herself.

Reciprocate an invitation to play at another child's
house with one to play at yours.

Do not force friendships because it is convenient
for you or because you are friends with the
other child's parents. Everyone should be
allowed to choose his or her friends.

Try This at Home

When my daughter has a friend over, unless it is an
overnight visit, the television is off limits, and if they
want to write or play games on the computer, I impose
a time limit of one hour. Otherwise, I would prefer
they *play* on their playdate, outside in the yard or in
the house. Remember, it is your daughter's house, too,
and she and her friends should not be confined to her
room. My daughter and her friends love to sit in our
small study and flip through our family photo albums.
As long as the rule is established and enforced that

your daughter is responsible for cleaning up after the playdate, then a parent should relax and go with the flow—and the mess—of bead making, face painting, or baking cookies, with adult supervision as necessary.

Some Good Advice

The old maxim, "two's company, three's a crowd," definitely applies to young girls. When my daughter started kindergarten, she instantly bonded with Lauren. Within a couple of days, the duo became a trio with the addition of Lily. The girls had a lot in common and were nearly inseparable. Thus, we were surprised when their kindergarten teacher warned us that the group dynamic in threesomes could sometimes be problematic. Sure enough, one day two of the three banded together and were hurtful to the third. We were shocked, as the behavior was so out of character for any of the girls. We all came to school and had a sit-down with the girls and their teacher, which ended with the girls running off hand in hand to play. I'd like to say they lived happily ever after, at least through the school year, but that was not the case. I can't explain it, but for girls the number three equals trouble. They remained friends, but until they were mature enough to resolve conflicts on their own we scheduled playdates as twosomes, rotating the participants, and reserved threesomes for occasions when the moms were present.

Chapter Six

SLEEPOVERS: FRIENDS AND RELATIVES

*L*ike many people in this mobile society, I live a fair distance from my immediate family. Soon after I announced my pregnancy, my mother bought a plane ticket to coincide with my planned delivery date, and thanks to my daughter's good timing, her grandmother met her before she was twenty-four hours old. About six months later, it was time to present her to the rest of my family.

My parents watched in amazement as we unloaded our Volvo wagon. Out came Joy in her car seat/carrier, the suitcases, a box of toys, the baby monitor, a portable crib/playpen, a high chair, a bouncy seat, a rolling seat, and a stroller. As we traversed across the great state of Texas, from one sibling's house to another, the ritual was repeated three more times. It was exhausting and would have been more practical to shoot lots of video, and let everyone come to us at their leisure.

As soon as your daughter begins to spend the night in other people's homes, she should be taught to respect other people's things and the rules in other people's homes.

Little girls, in general, are ready for sleepovers at an earlier age than little boys. However, they should not be spending the night out until at least the age of five. One of the great measures of independence in your daughter's life will be her first sleepover. When is she ready? It's easier to say when she is not.

She is not ready to sleep over at a friend's house if she is not sleeping through the night or if she is still wetting the bed. If you have the slightest doubt, it is not worth the humiliation your child will suffer waking up in a friend's home on a wet sheet. If your daughter has not had an incident in some time, and thinks she is ready, talk to her beforehand about what to do if an accident happens: she should inform the host parent rather than hurriedly make the bed, hide her nightclothes, and hope no one notices. It is up to her friend and the friend's parents to treat her with the compassion she deserves.

If it should happen in your home with a visiting child, assure her that accidents happen to everyone and get her into a clean set of clothes. Quickly get the children's minds off of it with a special breakfast, Saturday morning cartoons, or playtime outside. Have a private, thoughtful, and emphatic talk with your child at the soonest opportunity to be sure she understands that it was an accident, that her friend probably feels very embarrassed, and that it is not to be spoken of again. Invite that child over again soon to let her know that the accident is forgotten.

When your daughter is ready for a sleepover at a friend's house, she packs a small bag with the basics: nightclothes, clean underwear, a change of clothes, toothbrush, toothpaste, hairbrush, required medications, a sleep toy, and in some cases, a pillow and sleeping bag. She may also bring a book and one or two small toys, but not her entire collection of dolls and their accessories. My daughter never leaves home without her CD case and her camera, and most girls bring along grooming essentials such as foam soap and fruit-scented body lotion.

A young lady follows her host home's bedtime rules without whining. Young girls like to stay up late talking and giggling but should do so quietly so as not to keep everyone up.

The host parent leaves on some type of night-light that can guide a child to a bathroom should she wake up in the middle of the night. If she has a tendency to fall out of bed or sleepwalk, her parents should make this known. In the morning, a young lady eats breakfast with the family and gathers her things together so that she is ready to go when her parent arrives to pick her up.

If your daughter's guest wants to go home, do not make her feel ashamed of being homesick. Likewise, if your child is tentative about spending the night away, assure her that she can call you if she needs to.

My daughter was five the first time she had a sleepover at a friend's house. I got emotional as I packed her little bag, drove her over to her friend's house, and waved bye-bye—to her rapidly disappearing back as she raced off to play, completely thrilled at the idea of spending a night away from mom. I didn't hear a peep until the next day when her friend's mom brought her home, all smiles and full of stories about her great adventure. And that's a good thing; logically I knew that her independence was a healthy sign of her self-confidence and security. In my sentimental mother's eye, however, I was already seeing her loading up her compact car and heading off to college without a backward glance. Hopefully, when that day arrives, she will do it with the same sense of adventure and confidence that she took with her on her first sleepover.

Your Daughter Is Becoming a Young Lady If . . .

She doesn't spread her belongings all over the place when visiting another home.

She is on her best behavior, obeying her friend's parents.

She leaves the bathroom as she found it.

She does not touch or use things that do not belong to her.

She conforms to house rules and schedule.

She informs her hosts immediately if she has an accident of any kind.

She shows a guest around the house, and lets her know where the bathroom, telephone, and exits are located.

She asks her guest what she would like to do.

She does not make fun of her guest if she has an accident, sleeps with a "blankie," or suffers a sudden bout of homesickness.

She thanks her hostess for having her or thanks her guest for coming.

Parent Pointers

Have phone numbers of the guest's parents and
their whereabouts for the evening.

Leave the name of your child's physician and
preferred hospital if there is any potential
for an emergency and you cannot be
reached.

Share your child's allergies or medical
conditions (for example, the proper use of
an inhaler if your child has asthma).

Inform the host or hostess of any sleeping
problems your child might have: sleepwalking,
restlessness, early rising.

Let the host or hostess know that if your child
suffers an inconsolable bout of homesickness,
you are available by phone or to pick her up,
no matter the hour.

Single parents do not have the person they are
dating spend the night in their home when
their children's friends are present.

Try This at Home

In my house, there is not a weekend goes by that I do
not have at least one, often two, children spending
the night. During the week there are playdates and
friends coming by for dinner, and in the summer, I

sometimes lose track—for a moment anyway—of how many kids are upstairs or in the backyard. I am constantly finding strange clothes, books, toys, and even inhalers around my house. Rather than trying to figure out what belongs to which kid, I throw it all into a plastic tub marked "lost and found," and the children who visit here know to check it for misplaced items.

Some Good Advice

Some sleepovers are not as exciting as when our children visit friends or relatives. Another type of sleepover is when parents are separated or divorced. The trauma of the breakup of a marriage on children should not be underestimated. My ex-husband, children, and I attended a course called "Children Facing Divorce," in which children were encouraged to discuss their feelings among their peers—which were later shared with their parents. I had no idea that my children were deeply concerned about what I would do while they were at their father's.

If you are facing this situation, bring it up in advance with your children; they probably won't ask. Tell them that you will miss them, but that you plan to go to the movies/dinner/a concert with your friends (make it up if you have to) and that you know they will have a great time with their other parent. It would be a good idea to have a friend over the first time your child spends the night with the other parent in their new home. Take my word for it, it will be difficult, and you will need all the support you can get.

Chapter Seven

PARTY MANNERS

*B*irthdays were a big deal in my family. Before the big day, cards began arriving in the mail from distant relatives. My mother let me choose what kind of birthday cake I wanted. From the moment I opened my eyes in the morning, until my head hit the pillow that night, it was my "special" day. From the time I was about six, I had a small party at home with friends every other year, but not all parties are small.

When I was in first grade, I went to a very elegant party held in a huge house to which every girl in the class was invited. Wearing our best party dresses, we played orderly party games, then sat down at the long, gleaming dining room table for lunch served by a uniformed maid. As the grand finale, her father sat down at the piano to accompany us in singing "Happy Birthday," and her mother carried in the multitiered, professionally decorated cake.

I am of the opinion that children should not have big birthday parties until they are out of diapers. Do observe the special day with close family, and if your extended family does not live close by, perhaps invite another family with a child of the same age.

I also question the good sense of parents who plan extravagant celebrations for their toddlers. One party we attended for a two-year-old included sixteen children; there was also a clown, who terrified all sixteen children. At a party that my daughter attended for a friend turning three, the parents had hired a pony; Joy was the only one of eight little girls who would get on the horse.

No matter what kind of party she is invited to, it is unrealistic to expect anything but basic party manners from your child until she is about five years old, which is about the youngest that parents can drop their daughter off at a party. When dropping her off at a party, always check in with the parents. When your child receives an invitation to a birthday party, it is your responsibility to RSVP immediately, particularly if the party is planned for an establishment that must have a head count.

A young lady should be on time for a party. If she is going to be late because of a dance recital or a swimming lesson, let the host or hostess know ahead of time. Upon arrival, a young lady wishes the guest of honor a happy birthday and deposits her gift with the others. When it is time to open the gifts, a young lady does not thrust her present in the birthday girl's face but waits her turn. She does not make any snooty comments about the other gifts, and she never mentions the cost of a gift.

When the cake is presented, she does not wriggle her way into the seat beside the birthday girl but takes the first available place at the table. A guest does not assist in blowing out the candles unless it is requested, and she does not ask for a bigger slice of cake or the piece with the special décor. If she does not care for birthday cake, she asks for a very small piece and takes at least one bite in the spirit of the occasion.

When the party is over, she again tells the guest of honor happy birthday and thanks her and the parents for being included.

Birthday girls can assist with the planning of their parties as long as they have realistic expectations—taking her entire class to a theme park for the day is not realistic; taking one or two friends to a theme park for a day is. They can also assist with sending out invitations and assembling the party favors that are distributed to guests at the end of the party.

When her guests arrive, the birthday girl greets everyone, making them all feel welcome. When opening presents before an audience, the guest of honor acknowledges the giver, shows the opened gift to the audience, and offers a sincere thanks. She never says, "I don't play with Barbie anymore."

When it is time for cake, the birthday girl can help slice it if she desires; otherwise, she gets the first piece. When the party is over, she says good-bye to everyone, and thanks them for coming. Thank-you notes (see chapter 21) are sent within two weeks of the party.

Besides birthday parties, there will be other opportunities for young ladies to attend family-inclusive parties marking holidays from Christmas to the Fourth of July and joyous celebrations such as weddings. If children are invited to the wedding and reception, it will be noted on the invitation. If it is not, or if children are specifically asked to stay away, parents should get a babysitter or decline the invitation. In most cases, girls can wear what they would wear to church or temple. Children are not typically invited to formal seated affairs and seated and served dinners. They are, however, usually invited when there is a buffet. Children younger than six should not be permitted to carry their own plate through the buffet line. They can point out to their parent what they would like. Girls six and older can carry their own plates, but they do not treat a buffet like an all-you-can-eat breakfast bar. At a buffet there is no reason for a young lady to wait for everyone to be seated until she eats; she does not take her used plate back to the buffet for a second helping.

In private homes where seating is at a minimum, a young lady does not take a place that would prevent an adult from sitting, but can find a step on the staircase or a spot on the floor, as long as it is not in a walking path.

Your Daughter Is Becoming a Young Lady If . . .

She is considerate of other children who weren't invited or just didn't attend a party by not talking about the party.

She greets and bids farewell to the guest of honor, and thanks her and her parents for the invitation.

She makes an effort to include everyone in the fun and thanks every guest for coming.

She never tries to steal the spotlight at another girl's birthday party.

She participates in all the party activities that she can. By accepting the invitation, a young lady has made a tacit agreement to be a cheerful guest.

She does not ask for more of anything—drinks, pizza, popcorn, candy, cake, pony rides, laser tag games, or arcade tokens—unless it is offered.

She never says, "I already have this," when opening a present.

When and if a young gentleman is so bold as to ask her to dance, a young lady accepts graciously and does her best not to step on his toes.

Parent Pointers

Allow your daughter one guest per each year of her age; a five-year-old can invite five friends, a ten-year-old can ask ten.

Send party invitations in the mail, or via e-mail [or Evite], not to school in your daughter's backpack.

Be sure your daughter knows not to talk about her own party, or a friend's party, in front of other children who may not be invited.

Do not request that your daughter be allowed to bring her sibling or an out-of-town guest to a birthday party to which your daughter is invited.

If a dance recital or music lesson will delay your daughter's arrival at a birthday party by thirty minutes or more, be sure that a late arrival is all right with the hosts. If the delay would be longer than an hour, decline the invitation.

Keep track of who gave which gift so that your daughter can mention it in the thank-you note.

Be on time to pick up your daughter after the party, and make sure to tell the hosting parents that you are taking your child.

Let your daughter know that she is expected to eat whatever she puts on her plate at a buffet. That means only one dessert.

Let your daughter participate as much as possible in the planning, execution, and cleanup of the party her family is hosting.

Suggest ways that your daughter can be sure everyone feels comfortable and included, particularly children who don't know many other children there.

TRY THIS AT HOME

Birthday party hosts sometimes dispense party favors to guests at the end of the party, as a thank-you for coming. Toy and party stores always have an aisle devoted to "party favors," cheap plastic toys that are about as well made and long lasting as the useless promotional junk that fast-food chains dispense with their children's meals. There are also special party favor bags to put all the stuff into. Don't waste your money. If you want to distribute party favors, get one good and useful thing: a mini flashlight, a paperback book, or a sketch pad and marker, add a few lollypops and a pack of sugarless gum, and put it in a paper sack marked with each child's name. If my daughter comes home from a birthday party with a bulging bag of candy, it is subject to parental distribution.

Some Good Advice

When I was growing up, we spent a week every summer in a small community of cabins by a mountain lake. Every Saturday night, there was a square dance in the recreation hall. The summer I was twelve, I was sitting at a table with other girls in the camp when one of the boys walked determinedly across the dance floor, positioned himself in front of me, and asked me to dance. I wasn't terribly fond of this boy, and feeling quite full of myself, said, "No, thank you." As the other girls tittered, he shrank about two inches in height and crept away.

Seconds later, I felt my mother's fingernails digging into my arm as she hissed in my ear, "Come with me." Outside we went, where she let me have it. "Who do you think you are? How *dare* you turn that boy down when he walked all the way across the room in front of everyone to ask you to dance? Never turn down a man who asks you to dance. It is three minutes out of your life, and it won't kill you. Now you get your little fanny back in there and ask him to dance. And I won't be sorry for you if he says no."

So that's what I did, and he, being more considerate than me, said yes. We danced, and it didn't kill me. In fact, it was fun. I never again turned down a man who asked me to dance and have enjoyed every dance since.

Chapter Eight

DINING IN AND OUT

*I*nfants pretty much set their own pace when it comes to eating. The baby wakes up, cries, nurses (or takes a bottle), burps, sleeps, wakes up, cries, nurses, burps, sleeps, wakes up, cries, and on and on. At this stage, good dining manners are completely up to the mother. One school of thought is that since nursing is good for babies and a perfectly natural function, then it is appropriate in public places wherever and whenever the need arises, even if that is at the table in a busy restaurant. Others opt for a bit more discretion, retiring to another room for a few moments alone with the baby. Because nursing at a table in a restaurant, sitting in a dentist's waiting room, or in the pew at church might make others nearby uncomfortable, I opt for the latter course of action.

As the baby demands more and more feeding, the time comes to begin adding solid food to his or her diet. The Academy of American Pediatrics considers four to six months a good age to start. Table manners are still a long way off, and anyone who has watched an infant smear food all over herself can attest to that. Finger eating will continue for some time, and it isn't pretty, but it's a necessary step in the bumpy—and messy—road to independence. Give her a spoon, but don't expect her to use it as anything more than a toy or drumstick. It will take some time for your daughter, no matter how well developed her motor skills are, to develop a working relationship with her spoon and fork—eighteen months on average—and she will still switch back and forth between using a utensil and using her fingers. By the time your daughter is using a booster seat to take her place at the table, and using utensils more than not, the mastering of basic table manners is just a few simple lessons away.

Every young lady, as soon as she is able to reach a sink—even a three-year-old who requires the aid of a step stool—washes her hands before coming to the table. Once she is at the table, the simplest things go a long way. Even very young girls can be taught not to play with their food, not to chew with their mouths open, not to talk with their mouths full, and to keep their elbows off the table. If parents lead by example, and insist on these common courtesies with consistent reinforcement, they need not fear coarse behavior from their young lady when the family has company over, dines out, or when their daughter has dinner on her own at a friend's house.

The adoption of more complicated tools and sophisticated skills comes next. The napkin is not intended to be used as a hat, a kerchief, or a place to spit the peas you don't want to eat. A young lady places her napkin in her lap after being seated. Once the napkin is on the lap, it should be used to wipe one's mouth and fingers during and after the meal. If a napkin ring is used, a young lady places it on the table, not around her wrist like a bracelet or hooked to her ear like an earring. The knife is used only when she has reasonably mastered its use, otherwise food could be flying across the table. Once she is able to cut her own meat or butter her own biscuits, a young lady always places the dirty knife across her plate when not in use, not on the table.

No matter how utterly famished she is, a young lady waits until everyone is seated before digging into her food. In homes where grace is said, a young lady waits until after the blessing to begin eating.

If a young lady desires something that is out of her reach, she asks somebody to pass it to her, using "please" and "thank you," of course.

Young ladies should remember that, unless the meal is ordered from a restaurant, someone in the house—frequently the mother—has gone to some degree of effort to create the meal for her beloved family. A young lady never wrinkles her nose at the plate of food, nor does she say, "Eeeeew, what's this?" If she does, she should not be surprised if her mother removes her plate from the table and sends the little girl to her room.

DINING IN AND OUT

All parents, even the most sophisticated gourmands, will discover that young taste buds are narrowly defined, and for many years will only respond favorably to foods that can be covered with ketchup, tomato sauce, syrup, or melted cheese. Over time this will change, and a fondness for a greater variety of foods will develop with exposure to new foods. I subscribe to the notion of exposing children to new foods but not to the notion of making children eat everything on their plates. For reasons known to them alone, they have very distinct likes and dislikes predicated on everything from color to texture.

A young lady does not hunker down over her food, gobbling it as if it were her last meal, nor does she dillydally and push it about her plate. Instead, she maintains a reasonable pace by observing her fellow diners. When a young lady is finished eating, she may ask, "May I please be excused?" When permission is granted, she carries her plate to the kitchen counter unless she is told to leave it for clearing later.

Dining out with children in full-service restaurants is always an adventure, and one for which parents should be sure they and their offspring are ready. While many diners are apprehensive about children in a restaurant, entire families have every right to dine at family restaurants. Likewise, fellow diners have every right to expect those children to behave and not interfere with their dining enjoyment. Restaurants that employ maître d's, sommeliers, and Riedel stemware are probably not suited for children.

When dining out, not only do the same basic rules of the home table apply, but because there are other people around, young ladies also do not raise their voices at the table. They have good posture, and do not loll about on a banquette. They practice patience for, unlike in their own homes, there is always a wait for food in restaurants. Many family restaurants provide crayons, place mats, and small games to help children pass the interminable fifteen minutes of downtime, but parents should also be prepared with something even as simple as a small pad of paper.

Before a young lady attends her first formal dinner—in an upscale restaurant, at a party, or in a home—she should know the basic rules of bread plates, silverware, and passing:

- The bread plate is the smaller one to the left above the forks. (The salad plate is larger, and also to the left of the place setting.) Her beverage glass is to the right of her plate.

- A young lady takes one piece of bread and one pat of butter, then passes them to the right.

- Silverware is used from the outside in. When a course is completed, a young lady puts her used silverware on the plate.

- When serving dishes are being passed family-style, passing begins with the plate in front of you, and goes to the right around the table.

- When dining in someone's home, a young lady
  always says something nice about the meal
  and thanks her host or hostess. Unless there is
  professional help, she offers to help clear the table.

Your Daughter Is Becoming
a Young Lady If . . .

She washes her hands and removes her hat before
coming to the table.

She does not bring a cell phone or any other
electronic device to the table.

She keeps all four legs of her chair on the floor.

She keeps elbows off the table, does not chew with
her mouth open, or talk with her mouth full.

She does not play with her hair at the table.

She asks someone to pass the salt and pepper instead
of reaching across the table.

She does not take the last helping without offering it
to someone else.

When being served, she does not refuse a dish unless
she is allergic. Instead, she asks for a very small
amount.

She does not eat before the others begin, before her
host or hostess is seated, or before the blessing.

She asks to be excused from the table to go to the
restroom, or when she is finished eating.

She does not ask about dessert while everyone is still eating the salad.

When dining in a restaurant, she does not get up from the table and wander about.

She does not create bizarre and potentially explosive concoctions from the condiments on the table.

She keeps her hands and arms close to her body, being careful not to spill or drop beverages and food on the floor.

She treats the server cordially and with respect, saying "thank you" when her meal is delivered, and her plate is taken away.

Parent Pointers

Teach by example and consistently follow basic dining etiquette.

Do not expect children to master the use of a fork and spoon until about the age of four. A knife is some way down the road.

Be patient when your daughter has accidents at the table. If she is big enough, let her clean up the spill herself.

Encourage your daughter to taste different foods, but don't make her eat it if she doesn't like it.

Never argue at the dinner table.

Do not have the television on during dinner (unless a once-in-a-lifetime historical event is being broadcast—the first astronaut landing on Mars, or the Chicago Cubs winning the World Series).

If the home phone rings during dinner, keep it short, and promise to return the call after the meal.

Do not talk on your cell phone at a table in a restaurant. If you must take the call, go outside.

Treat servers and professional help with respect. If the meal or service is not satisfactory, make your complaints discreetly to the manager.

Always compliment and thank the host or hostess when invited to dine in another's home.

TRY THIS AT HOME

I have found that making a habit of using cloth napkins promotes their proper use. Going one step further, don't reserve the best china, silver, and stemware for company, holidays, or special celebrations. If you want your daughter to be comfortable with the protocol of formal dining, occasionally break the habit of dinner in the kitchen. Set up in the dining room, pulling out all the fancy linens, china, silver, stemware, and serving pieces. Don't wear yourself out with the Julia Child cookbook; meat loaf and mashed potatoes will do just fine.

Some Good Advice

Do not force children to eat something they have tried and hate. My mother, a child of the Depression, believed you ate whatever was set before you—all of it. Every night for dinner we had meat, a starch, and a vegetable. The only vegetables any of us five children liked were corn, salad, raw carrots, applesauce, and cranberry sauce (the last two counted as vegetables in our family). We especially despised peas. My father always had a loaf of white bread sitting at his end of the table. One evening after a dinner that included peas, we all cleaned our plates quite nicely and were scooted outside to play while my mother cleaned up. The next morning, we were eating breakfast while she made lunches for school that day. We heard her make a retching noise and all of us—except one sister—ran out to the kitchen. There in the loaf of bread, two slices back from the front, were my sister's peas from the night before. The pea juice had seeped through the spongy loaf of white bread, ruining every piece. My mother was pretty mad, but looking at all our faces, waiting to see what would happen next, she finally burst out laughing at my sister's ingenuity. We had peanut butter crackers in our lunch boxes that day, and never again had to choke down a vegetable that we hated.

Chapter Nine

CULTURAL AFFAIRS:
THE THEATER, MOVIES,
SPORTS, MUSEUMS, AND
LIBRARIES

When my daughter was four years old, I took her to a matinee performance of *The Nutcracker* by the city ballet company at the performing arts center. Our seats were fifteen rows back from the stage, right in the center. I thought being close would keep her engaged in the performance. She had been taking ballet at the community arts center for about a year and was immediately enthralled by the dancers, the music, and the costumes. The male and female leads were about midway through a very dreamy ballet in the first act, and except for the orchestra, the entire theater was silent, held in rapt attention. Suddenly, out of nowhere, my daughter asked—loudly enough to be heard in a five-row radius: "Mommy, is he wearing any underwear?" Given the costume, it was an obvious question, and stated so sweetly that everyone who heard it had to do their best to stifle their laughter. Thankfully, the matinee was one marketed specifically to children, and such a faux pas was not unprecedented.

In all fairness to Joy, I probably had not prepared her well enough for a live performance. Prior to that, her experience as a member of an audience had been limited to sixty-minute animated films in loud, baby- and children-filled cineplexes, story hours in the children's section of bookstores and public libraries, baseball games, and the occasional puppet show. Still, even the most youth-oriented productions require at least a minimal level of manners and respect for other audience members.

Once little girls are mobile and talking, parents should enforce audience etiquette during the performance, no matter how many unruly heathens are running about. If your young lady remains in her seat, and does not inhibit the viewing enjoyment of others by standing up or their listening pleasure by talking, perhaps others will follow her lead.

If she has seen the movie before, she does not tell her friends the ending, nor does she announce a crucial scene: "Ooooo, this is where she finds out that her new friend is actually her twin sister!" A young lady does not throw Raisinettes at her friend sitting two rows in front of her to get her attention, slurp on a straw, crunch ice loudly, or rest her food and drink in the row where she might inadvertently kick it over. When the movie is over, a young lady picks up her trash and deposits it in the garbage can located by the door of the theater.

As your young lady gets older, she will have occasion to frequent performances, events, and cultural institutions that require more refined manners and a more mature level of behavior. The first step in promoting good audience manners is making certain a girl is old enough to enjoy the experience. If a girl is adamant about not wanting to attend the symphony, don't force the issue. Good behavior comes naturally when a child is enchanted by what is taking place before her. A young lady may never develop a passion for the opera, but if she is in the audience, she is expected to exhibit a healthy respect for the efforts and skills of the artists and craftsmen behind the production.

Children's theater is a wonderful introduction to the stage; the productions are lively, often including audience participation, and more importantly, are short. Alfresco theater, such as Shakespeare in the Park, is another fine way to ease children into the pleasures of the play; if the dialogue sails over their heads, restless young ladies can occupy themselves by lying on their backs and gazing at the stars.

Once you determine that your child is old enough to sit relatively still for two to three hours and plans are made to attend a play, the opera, a symphony, or the ballet, a young lady should be told what to expect, and what is expected of her.

For a live production of any type, members of

the audience arrive on time in order to be seated before the performance begins; it is exceedingly rude to come in after the curtain has risen. If they are tardy, they must wait quietly in the back of the theater until an usher finds the opportunity to seat them. A young lady visits the restroom and the water fountain before being seated. If her seat is in the center of the row, and others are already seated, she says excuse me as she approaches them and allows them to stand or shift their knees to let her pass. In either case, she must be very conscious not to step on any toes. She passes facing them, with her back against the seats in the other row. If she is already seated and someone needs to move past her, she should tuck her feet under her chair and make sure the floor is clear in front of her.

She typically will not be permitted to bring food or drink into a theater or performance hall. During intermission, she may go to the lobby with her parents or host or hostess and enjoy a refreshment if it is offered to her.

A young lady does not talk during the performance. If she must ask a question, she whispers into the ear of her mother or father. Even if she is miserably bored, a young lady does not emit extravagant and dramatic sighs of ennui, and she covers her mouth when she yawns, lest she start an epidemic. She does not flip loudly through the program or use it as a fan. She doesn't wiggle in her seat, swing her legs, or kick the seat in front of her; nor does she fling her hair about or stand up. She follows the lead of the adults in applauding and standing for an ovation.

Attending a sporting event is a great opportunity to admire the skills of highly trained and disciplined athletes. I have been taking my daughter and son to baseball games since they were still in strollers. Though staged in a more casual setting than the opera, there is still protocol to observe at sporting events. Young ladies get to their seat without disturbing their fellow spectators, being careful not to hit anyone in the eye with a souvenir hockey stick or knock over a beverage that her parent must offer to replace. She keeps her belongings in her lap or under her seat. She stands for the singing of the national anthem, always removing her hat if she is wearing one. Once the game begins, a young lady sits and remains seated unless a spectacular play occurs and all her neighbors stand for a better look.

It is fine to stand, stretch, and move about between quarters or periods. With respect to her fellow spectators, during play of the game, a young lady does not get up to go to the restroom or concession stands, or try to return to her seat from doing so. Instead, she waits for a natural break in the action. A young lady does not scatter the remnants of her food and beverage about her; no one wants to step into a pile of nachos. Instead, she keeps her food on her lap while eating it, then puts the trash under her seat until she can deposit it in a garbage can.

In spite of the unseemly behavior of many grown-ups that would indicate otherwise, buying a ticket to a sporting event does not entitle a young lady to scream insults at the players on the opposite team.

There are other cultural venues where a young lady will have the chance to practice her developing good manners. When visiting a library, a young lady is quiet, respects others, and has a certain reverence for the institution itself. If she is looking at or reading books in the library, she does not remove more than she needs from the shelves. When she is finished with her books, she returns them to the book cart and does not try to re-shelve them herself. If there are computers available, she does not monopolize them to play games or e-mail musical greeting cards to all her classmates when others may need them for more pressing purposes such as doing research or writing a résumé.

In museums other than those geared specifically to small children, she moves quietly and calmly from room to room in the normal flow of traffic. She stands far enough back from the exhibit to allow others to see. She does not read the descriptions of the pieces aloud unless she is assisting a nonreader, in which case she should do it as quietly as possible. She does not touch paintings, sculptures, or other museum pieces. She does not lie down on the benches for a quick snooze, no matter how bored she may be.

Your Daughter Is Becoming a Young Lady If . . .

She sits quietly and attentively through a performance, without fidgeting or napping.

She disposes of her chewing gum before going into a theater for a live performance.

She cleans up her space in a movie theater when the film concludes.

She doesn't cheer when a member of an opposing team is hurt.

She does not boo her own team no matter how inept their play.

She does not berate spectators who are rooting for the other team and does not gloat if her team wins.

She does not knock anyone over while racing to get a ball hit into the stands, nor does she grapple with others over T-shirt or candy bar giveaways.

She sits in her seat on her bottom, not on her knees or feet, or perched on the armrest.

She does not stand and block the view of the people behind her, lest they miss a last-second three pointer that will be talked about for weeks.

She does not make untoward or uninformed remarks—"That's stupid; I could have painted that!" about the art she is viewing in a museum or gallery. The audio tour of the exhibit would probably be enthusiastically received by children accustomed to headphones.

Parent Pointers

Do not force cultural expeditions on your daughter until she is ready to sit still for the duration.

Arrive on time for the performance.

Teach your daughter to respect the performers and fellow audience members.

Turn your beepers and cell phones to vibrate before entering a theater or leave them in the car.

Do not text or check your e-mails on your mobile device during a performance.

Make sure bathroom needs are attended to before being seated, and check to be sure chewing gum has been disposed of properly.

Carry a cough drop or throat lozenge in case the need arises; if an uncontrollable coughing fit begins, leave the theater as unobtrusively and quickly as possible.

Take out of the theater what you brought into the theater.

Never take small children to movies that are
  clearly intended for adults. If you cannot retain
  a babysitter, wait for another night or rent the
  video.

Do not get into an argument with another
  audience member or spectator over their bad
  behavior; instead, inform an usher and he or
  she will take care of it.

Exhibit good sportsmanship at sporting events,
  resisting the urge to point out a player's
  shortcomings, boo bad plays, or drink too
  much beer.

When watching a golf game or tennis match, be
  aware of the more stringent rules of spectator
  etiquette.

TRY THIS AT HOME

When I was growing up, there were few professional
women athletes and few school-sanctioned female
athletics. Title IX legally changed that, but amateur
and professional female sports still do not receive
the same rabid response as men's sports. You can do
your part to support female athletes by taking your
daughter to a woman's basketball or soccer game; treat
them and their competitions with the same respect
you accord the male athletes.

SOME GOOD ADVICE

Many performing arts organizations have auxiliary groups, such as the Opera Guild, or Friends of the Ballet. Within those groups, there is often a club expressly for children, such as our symphony's Pied Piper Club. There is at least one performance a year geared specifically for the children. Group members usually sit together and enjoy a little ice cream or cookie reception afterward. Parents who wish to cultivate in their daughter an interest in the arts might consider a membership in such a group. They are typically inexpensive and usually include the price of a ticket to a performance.

Chapter Ten

TRAVELING MANNERS

*O*ne week before my daughter started
kindergarten in August 1995, I bought a new
car. That milestone in her life—and mine—also
signaled the advent of her social career and my taxi
service. By the end of the school year in May 2001,
I had put 87,575 miles on that car, an average of
15,000 miles a year, which doesn't seem like a lot, but
those miles were logged in a fifteen-mile radius of
my home, driving my children—and any number of
their friends—to and from school, sporting events,
lessons, meetings, birthday parties, playdates, camp,
swim clubs, pediatricians, and dentists. Day after day,
I see the same women on the same route; we wave at
one another as we pass, each tucked within our auto
cocoon, filled with our precious little charges.

Moms' cars are easily identified; they're the ones
with parking permit stickers on the rear bumper, a

tangle of sporting equipment in the rear cargo space, and an interior resembling Woodstock after the masses had departed.

It occurred to me one day that like most mothers I drive and drive and drive, and basically I go nowhere. It was not a heartening thought. Within that context, good traveling manners are important so that the driving mother isn't pushed over the edge. When squabbles arise in my car, as they do on a regular basis, I pull over to the first safe spot, turn off the ignition, and read the backseat riders the riot act. My sister, who has four children and was always transporting at least twice that many in her Econo-van, used to carry a wooden spoon; when things got particularly chaotic in the van, she would pick up the spoon and flail it in the general direction of the second-row occupants. It was an effective warning device.

Just a generation ago, the deregulation of the airline industry made flying accessible to nearly everyone. Before that, families went on vacation or to visit relatives in a car. As long as the eventual destination was reachable by some combination of blacktop, gravel, and dirt road, then the automobile was the way to go. Although airplanes don't offer much more space or freedom of movement than a car, once travel moves from within the private confines of the family auto to the public world of airplanes— buses, subways, trains—courtesy and self-control become crucial. A lack of personal space over an extended period of time can cause even grown-ups to forget their manners, which, at its worst, can result in something the airline industry refers to as "air rage." This dangerous behavior does not refer to squalling babies or smart-aleck children, but grown-ups throwing temper tantrums. Still, most adults regard a mother carrying a baby or hauling children down the aisle of a plane with the same dread they would a crazy-eyed zealot; please, please, please, in the name of God, don't let them sit anywhere near me.

My own experience of the trials and tribulations of traveling with my daughter and son has imbued me with compassion for all parents traveling with small children, but not so much that I would patiently tolerate rude behavior from a child. In such confined space, it is crucial that parents strictly enforce courteous behavior from their offspring.

The advent of more affordable airfare has had the unfortunate side effect of introducing a more casual approach to air travel. I am not lobbying for a return to the days of suit and tie, hats and gloves, but I would vote for the prohibition of grown men traveling in shorts, tank tops, and shower shoes, and nubile teenage girls dressed like streetwalkers. What are these people thinking? And what kind of example are they setting? Unless the flight is a red-eye, or a very lengthy international flight, children should not wear their pajamas on board. A young lady should be appropriately attired in something she might wear to school.

A young lady follows all instructions when boarding, never cutting in line. She assists her overloaded parents by carrying her own bags. While maneuvering the slim aisle of an aircraft, a young lady is aware of other passengers trying to jam their carry-on bags into the overhead compartment or under their seats. She does not squeeze past them but waits until they are seated to move along. At her row, she stows her carry-ons as quickly as possible, taking her seat to allow other passengers to pass. If a passenger in her row comes along after she is seated, a young lady gets up to let that person get to their seat.

While some airlines have recently widened the seats and added more leg room, the fact remains that they are still confined quarters. Young ladies do not sprawl in their seats, nor do they hog the armrests. Though most airline seats can be moved to a reclining position, a young lady should keep her seat upright to be considerate of the person behind her. If she must put her seat back, she should ask the person whose space she will be invading. Children have no reason to employ the reclining position, and they do not ever kick the back of the seat in front of them.

Young ladies respond politely when spoken to by a fellow passenger, but opening a book or putting on headphones can subtly signal that she would prefer not to carry on a lengthy conversation about her grades and extracurricular activities. She does not spread out her books and sketch pads and markers on the seat beside her; instead, she uses the seat pocket in front of her and only takes out what she needs at any given time. A young lady does not call the harried flight attendant for frivolous matters, nor does she ask the flight attendant to bring her more ice or change her turkey sandwich for ham. She does not ask a fellow passenger if he or she is going to eat his or her cookie. A young lady uses headphones if she is listening to something on her computer. If she is listening to an iPod, she does not crank up the volume, sing along with the music, or bounce to the beat. She turns all sound off while emergency procedures are being outlined and when taking off and landing.

When the plane lands, a young lady resists the urge to imitate fellow passengers who do not believe rules apply to them. She remains seated until the plane is secured at the gate, and the "fasten seat belt" sign is turned off. She retrieves her carry-on items so that she is ready to go when her turn comes. If someone near her is struggling with bags, she offers to help. She does not barge past other passengers. At the luggage carousel, a young lady does not push in front of others to get her bag.

If your daughter is going to be flying solo to visit a relative or noncustodial parent, you must thoroughly prepare her beforehand. Tell her what will be expected of her, and go over all the above rules of safe and courteous travel. Make every effort to see that she is not seated in the very rear of the plane, but close to the front. Be sure she knows that while rules of talking to strangers are relaxed on an airplane, if a fellow passenger says or does anything inappropriate, or makes her uncomfortable in any way, she should get up from her seat and privately inform a flight attendant immediately. She should never go with anyone who has not been pre-authorized by you, even if that person says you have sent him or her. Most airlines allow children twelve and under to fly only nonstop flights when traveling alone.

When staying at a hotel, a young lady remembers that she is not the only guest. She does not treat the lobby as a gymnasium, or ride up and down in the glass elevator as if it were an amusement park ride. When boarding an elevator, she waits until all disembarking passengers exit, then she punches the button for her floor and moves to the back of the elevator. If she is closest to the control panel, she holds the doors for others and asks them what floor they would like. She does not punch all the buttons on an elevator, nor does she push the alarm or "emergency stop" button to see what will happen. She does not place a call on the elevator emergency phone.

In her room, she remembers that there are other guests beside, above, and below her. She does not jump on the bed; turn up the television or radio exceedingly loud; bounce a ball off the floor, ceilings, or walls; slam drawers and doors; or roughhouse with her siblings.

When riding in a taxi, a young lady gets in first and slides across the seat, saving less agile adults the trouble. She allows the adult to give the driver their destination, and does not make fun of the driver's accent or name posted on his license. At their destination, she leaves the cab on the side away from traffic, and checks to be sure she has all her belongings.

When taking public transportation, a young lady has her fare or ride ticket ready at the train turnstile or door of the bus so as not to delay other riders. She takes a seat if one is available; if one is not, she finds a way to secure her position so that sudden movements do not send her flying into another rider's lap. If she has a seat on a full bus, and an elderly person or woman with small children boards, a young lady gets up and offers her seat. When her stop is imminent, a young lady prepares to disembark and moves through the mass without shoving, using "excuse me" as needed.

When going through a door, a young lady makes sure not to allow the door to slam on the person behind her but holds it open for that person. If she is strong enough, a young lady can open the door for others and let them pass through. A young lady does not play in revolving doors or trap someone inside. She does not push them around so quickly that someone might get hurt.

Your Daughter Is Becoming
a Young Lady If . . .

She shows respect and courtesy toward the parent
driving the car pool and does not engage in
backseat verbal or physical jousting.

She removes all her belongings from the car pool
vehicle.

She does not talk on her cell phone in the car
pool vehicle unless it is an emergency and she
informs the driver first.

She does not leave juice boxes, empty chip bags, or
gum wrappers on the floor or seat of the car.

When flying, she presents a neat appearance and
maintains control of her belongings.

She thanks the flight attendant who brings her
a beverage and snack, and she gives back her
beverage cup and other trash when asked.

She makes appropriate use of the pillows and
blanket offered by the flight attendant, and
does not confuse her seat for a bed.

She does not take more than her share of space or
recline her seat into the lap of the passenger
behind her.

She does not try repeatedly to open a bathroom
door that is clearly occupied.

She leaves the lavatory in better condition than she
found it.

She does not bring messy foods or ones with very strong odors on a plane.

She keeps the volume of her iPod or computer at a level only she can hear and turns it off during take-off or landing.

Parent Pointers

Set clear and defined ground rules for the occupants of your car pool; these apply to your own children as well as other children.

Do not talk or text on your cell phone while you are driving.

Keep a bag in your car for trash.

Do not apply makeup, shave, read, or eat anything that might impede your driving while you are behind the wheel.

Present a neat appearance and maintain control of your belongings and your children when traveling by plane, train, or bus.

Explain the basics of airport security to your children and monitor the contents of their carry-on luggage to be sure there is nothing that will cause a delay or undue alarm from security personnel.

Do all you can to secure seats together so that your children are sitting with you, not the nice lady ten rows back.

Bring along easy-to-carry diversions for small girls, and allow an older girl to pack her own backpack.

Do not bury your head in a book or put on the headphones and tune out your children. The flight attendant is not a babysitter.

Do not assume a girl under six can master the intricacies of an airplane bathroom by herself; go with her. Remind girls over six to clean up after themselves.

Present a good example to your children by following air industry policies and regulations, no matter how frustrated you may be by canceled flights, lost luggage, and snippy personnel.

Do not succumb to horn blowing, ranting, vulgar physical gestures, or other unmistakable signs of road rage in the car.

Instruct your daughter to stand up to offer her seat on a crowded bus or subway.

Always open doors for the elderly and mothers pushing strollers or carrying babies.

TRY THIS IN THE CAR

If you have two children in your car pool who do not get along, it can make the five-mile drive between home and school feel like a cross-country marathon. If possible, separate the two with a neutral child in between, or put one in the front seat if their size and an airbag does not prevent the arrangement. This will cut down on poking, pinching, and punching. If a battle ensues anyway, pull the car over at the first available safe place. Issue this warning: "If the behavior continues, no matter who was the instigator, both of you will be penalized." (I favor confinement to their room and no after-school snack.) If both children manage to get along for an entire week, I reward their mature behavior with a Friday-afternoon stop at a local market for a treat.

Some Good Advice

You never know when a traffic jam on the highway, inclement weather, equipment problems, or cancellations will add hours to your travel time. It is always wise to be prepared. In the backseat pockets of my car, I keep some travel games, crossword puzzles, word search books, and sketch pads for hangman or tic-tac-toe. I also have at least one book on tape, as well as Spanish on tape (a horizon-broadening moment never hurts). For long-distance travel, I let each child choose books and games for their backpacks, along with a couple of snacks—granola bars, an apple, goldfish—and a pack of sugarless gum. In my tote bag, I include some additional packs of peanut butter crackers and dried fruit in the event we are stuck on a runway for more than a few hours.

Chapter Eleven

BATHROOM HABITS, BEAUTY PRODUCTS, AND PERSONAL GROOMING

*W*hen my daughter was not quite six years old, she was invited to a "Beauty Parlor Birthday." A little alarm went off in my head; at that point, she was far more interested in balls than beauty products, and that suited me just fine. I estimate that from the time we enter our teens until the day we are laid out in our coffins, most women spend about ten years of their lives, and the equivalent of the gross national product of several small countries, adorning themselves. It seems to me there should be a period of immunity in a young girl's life—between birth and pimples—when she is primping-free. However, after that Beauty Parlor Birthday my daughter got the bug. Over the next few years, with each birthday, Christmas, and trip to the mall, her collection of products grew and grew and by the time she turned double digits, she had accumulated enough beauty aids to last a lifetime.

She and my son share a bathroom and a vanity with two sinks. Apparently the drawers below the counter are strictly for show because everything ends up on the counter. On my son's side of the border is an additional toothbrush, three combs, one brush, a cup, his toothpaste, floss, and a large bottle of L.A. Looks Mega Humidity Resistant Styling Gel.

On my daughter's side of the border is one brush, one comb, two bandannas, a visor, a macramé headband, Sparkling Green Apple Body Cream, Sun-ripened Raspberry Body Lotion, Sun-ripened Raspberry Shower Gel, Sun-ripened Raspberry Body Splash, Raspberry Sorbet Body Spray, Melon Mania Glitter Splash, Melon Mania Glitter Lotion, Blazin' Blueberry Glitter Splash, Blazin' Blueberry Shimmering Hair Gel, Sweet Honesty Bubble Bath, Sweet Honesty Body Splash, glow-in-the-dark glitter for hair and body, Funky Friends Body Glitter, an Old Navy bath fizzie, a blue and a purple roll-on glitter lip gloss, Smackers cosmic purple glitter nail polish, five bars of scented soap, a bag of multicolored ponytail holders, a tangle of beaded bracelets and necklaces, Caribbean Cool Deodorant bar, toothpaste, floss, original ChapStick, and a box of Stridex face wipes.

All this for a committed tomboy. I can't imagine the collection of a girlie-girl, as we call those who prefer dresses to jeans and Barbie dolls to kick balls.

A young lady should keep all her products in one place—if they can't fit in a basket or plastic tub, the surplus can be stored under the sink, or discarded. When she travels with products, she screws the lids on tightly and keeps them in a plastic ziplock bag to prevent spillage onto clothing.

A young lady does not spray herself with so much Sun-ripened Raspberry Body Splash that she attracts bees. She particularly does not over-scent herself if she is going to be in a confined space with captive companions. She does not spray herself with so much glitter that she resembles a disco ball or use so much gloss that she can't part her lips. A young lady learns the axiom "Less is more" early on.

Young ladies do not comb their hair at the table or just about anywhere else in public. Hair styling should be reserved for bathrooms, bedrooms, and powder rooms. A young lady does not monopolize a shared bathroom for a lengthy grooming routine. A young lady does not paint her nails in a common area of the home or in public places, such as waiting rooms or lounges; the odor is offensive and can cause headaches in others.

Nowhere is the great gulf between the genders wider than in how each sex attends to the need to go to the bathroom, belch, pass gas, remove an object from the nose, or relieve an itch in an intimate area. Generally, girls treat such needs privately. A young girl may very well be capable of belching the alphabet, but she never shows off that particular talent in public.

In general, television programs and movies have become more vulgar, particularly with bathroom and gross-out humor. Yet, even without exposure to wide-screen glorification of what is better carried out behind closed doors—or at least with some discretion—children cannot help but laugh at any bodily function that makes noise. Belching and passing gas are natural, and a young lady should not be made to feel ashamed if she accidentally does so in the company of others.

If a young lady accidentally belches or passes gas in public or in a small group, the mild offense can be resolved by simply saying "Excuse me"; no elaboration is necessary. If someone else passes gas or belches, a young lady does not laugh uproariously, point fingers, and try to further embarrass the offender. If a young lady knows she is going to belch, she keeps her lips pressed together to prevent a cacophonous expulsion. If she feels the dire need to pass gas, a young lady excuses herself and goes to the bathroom or a secluded area.

When a young lady uses a toilet, she closes the door. If it is a public restroom, she uses a seat cover, if they are available, before sitting. Some parents teach their daughters to crouch over a public toilet seat, never actually sitting upon it. Others use a length of toilet paper to wipe the seat before sitting. In any event, if after using the toilet, a young lady has gotten the seat wet, she wipes it dry with a piece of toilet paper. She flushes after use, then always washes her hands. A young lady uses a towel rather than the bottom half of her T-shirt for drying, and she places the towel back where she found it or puts discarded paper towels in the trash; the general vicinity of the trash can does not count.

Everyone, at one time or another, feels the need to remove something from his or her nose. Even in private, young ladies should execute discretion by using a tissue.

Scratching and spitting are two habits of questionable taste that are also nearly always the exclusive domain of the male gender. Both seem to have something to do with professional male athletes, who engage in these practices not only regularly, but also frequently on television and JumboTron and with little regard for modesty or decorum.

Your Daughter Is Becoming a Young Lady If . . .

She squelches her belches in public.

She leaves the room if she feels the need to pass gas.

She says "Excuse me" if she should unexpectedly or unavoidably do either of the above in the company of others.

She leaves the bathroom as clean as she found it.

She always washes her hands after using the bathroom.

She uses a small amount of air freshener if one is available when her visit to the bathroom results in a lingering odor.

She does not stay in the bathroom for extended periods of time, particularly if someone else is waiting.

She does not groom or style herself in public.

She uses modest amounts of beauty products.

She keeps all her beauty products together on her side of the sink when sharing a bathroom.

She uses a tissue or handkerchief when clearing her nose.

Parent Pointers

Employ the same good personal habits you seek from your daughter.

Urge children in your home to wash their hands after going to the bathroom. Good hygiene is good manners.

Be aware of the vulgar nature of some children's programming and make informed decisions about what humor you want your children exposed to.

Do not laugh at belching, passing gas, or vulgar humor.

Try This At Home

Even before she asks, parents should determine the age that their daughter will be allowed to pierce her ears, shave her legs, and wear makeup. With regard to the first two, my policy is that when she is old enough to handle the care of the pierced ears and the razor herself, then she is old enough to start. I set ten as the age for ear piercing, and twelve for leg shaving. By the time she turned ten, Joy had decided she was not interested in having her ears pierced, but she knows the option is available to her any time she changes her mind. She is looking forward to shaving her legs, at least until she discovers the maintenance involved. As far as makeup is concerned, anything more than lip gloss will not be allowed until she is thirteen. After that, peer pressure and advertising take over, and the best parents can do is take their daughter to a professional makeup counter so she can learn correct application and the value of good products.

Some Good Advice

Young boys and girls go through a stage—sometimes a very long stage—of finding potty talk very amusing. This is not alarming, but it is vulgar and discourteous. One friend found a surefire way to stop this kind of talk from her children. If they engage in potty talk, they are put in the bathroom for time-out. They are made to sit on the closed toilet seat for whatever period of time the infraction calls for. If they engage in potty talk at the dinner table, their plate is taken into the bathroom, and they finish the meal there. She reports this to be amazingly effective.

Chapter Twelve

MODESTY, BOUNDARIES, AND APPROPRIATE ATTIRE

*E*very family photo collection has an adorable picture of your naked infant getting a bath in the baby tub or perhaps the kitchen sink, her toothless smile a mile wide. Toddlers of both sexes splash happily together in a tub under a parent's watchful and amused eye—making bubbles, pouring water over each other's head with tub toys, and making soapy foam beards.

It's hard to pinpoint that Adam-and-Eve-in-the-Garden-of-Eden moment when a girl becomes self-conscious of her nudity, and giggles in the tub turn to shrieks of dismay should she be caught in the slightest state of undress. When that happens, the message is loud and clear. As sad as you may feel that the distinct line between innocent childhood and the first glimmers of awkward adolescence has been crossed, your daughter's emerging modesty and growing need for privacy must be respected and never dismissed or laughed at.

Before your daughter starts preschool, explain to her in a relaxed but firm tone what "private parts" and "inappropriate touching" mean. By nature, children are curious and exploratory. They also want to please others, particularly grown-ups they like and trust. She needs to hear from her parents—with reinforcement from the pediatrician on annual checkups—what is normal and appropriate, what is not, how to say "no," and when to tell a grown-up something has happened.

Conversations about reproduction and human sexuality are an ongoing process, and are subjects that should be addressed openly, honestly, positively—and appropriate to their age. There is no reason to have the same conversation with an eight-year-old that you would with an eighteen-year-old. Six-year-old girls will be confused and frightened by the mechanics of menstruation; eleven- and twelve-year-old girls who are close to starting their periods need information on what, when, why, and how to manage. Calling it "the Curse" will shed an unnecessarily negative light on something that is a natural function of the female body, and something they will be living with for many decades to come.

If you are uncomfortable or anxious about the topic, practice what you want to say, or think in advance of how you might answer certain questions.

Get a book on the subject, search the Internet, and talk to parents of girls who are a bit older than yours and get their advice.

Girls develop at different ages, and early or late, it is a challenging time for mother and daughter. Even before she has anything to put into a bra, your daughter will likely want something between her skin and her T-shirts, blouses, sweaters, and dresses. Way back when I was a preadolescent, we wore something called "training bras," which seemed logical at the time, but is hilarious in hindsight. Training? For what? Breasts?

As I discovered when I took Joy on that first "we need something for that stage between nothing and a real brassiere" exploratory shopping trip, there is no longer any such thing as "training bras." What I did find in a store targeted to preteen girls was more eye opening: padding and underwire. For twelve-year-olds! I was appalled at not only the unnecessary sexualizing of such young women, but the message that what they have needs lifting and supplementation. I probably didn't need to get on my soapbox about it to the two eighteen-year-old clerks behind the counter. My daughter, who was hiding in embarrassment behind a rack of sweatshirts, certainly wished she could drop through the floor.

I should have skipped that step, and let that be a warning to you should you feel so tempted to publicly express your indignation. Instead, go with your daughter to the underwear section of a department store or one that specializes in athletic wear. Tank tops, knit camisoles with lycra, and sports bras are a perfect solution for those transitional tween years.

Girls begin to acquire their own sense of style even before they develop. My daughter was always sporty, wearing clothes and shoes that allowed her to jump right into a foot race, kick ball or basketball game. Some young ladies are more girlie, and prefer skirts to shorts, dresses to jeans, pretty sandals to sneakers.

Whatever "type" your daughter is, help her to process the relentless barrage of impossible perfection and overt sexualizing from the media. Magazines, television shows, movies, music videos, and advertisements are all culpable. As long as you are purchasing the clothing, you have the authority to say "no" to a skirt that barely covers a rear end, a pair of jeans so low cut half her bottom shows when she sits down, a midriff-baring top, a T-shirt with an inappropriate message, or a skimpy bathing suit. And overly padded bras.

Young ladies should know how to wear a dress. Little girls do not pull their dresses up over their bellies to show their underwear, no matter how cute it is. Young ladies do not bend over from the waist while wearing a skirt or dress; when seated, they keep their knees and ankles together or cross their legs.

A young lady outfits herself in compliance with her school's dress code. A young lady doesn't exposes herself in a provocative manner, no matter how salaciously her favorite teenage pop singer is dressing, or not dressing.

Your Daughter Is Becoming a Young Lady If . . .

She always knocks on a closed door, particularly one that leads to a bathroom or bedroom.

She does not show her private parts to others, nor does she ask them to show theirs.

A young lady does not touch other children on their private parts, ask them to touch hers, or allow them to touch hers.

A young lady does her personal sexual exploration in the privacy of her bedroom or bathroom.

She does not use vulgar slang words for body parts.

She does not make offensive and inappropriate remarks about another person's looks or body.

When wearing a dress, a young lady keeps her knees closed when seated, and dips from the knees to reach something on the floor.

If her school has a dress code, she follows it.

Parent Pointers

Knock on your daughter's bedroom or bathroom door before entering, unless there are clear sounds or smells of distress or danger.

Make your daughter aware that the bathroom is a room where privacy must be respected.

Respect your daughter's privacy unless there is obvious distress or some imminent danger involved.

Offer your daughter accurate and nonthreatening sexual education in a timely and nonjudgmental fashion.

Be open and receptive to questions your daughter may have about her and others' sexuality.

Expect that your daughter will likely prefer to have this conversation with her mother.

Do not make up answers or pass on false information about sex (for example, "masturbation will make you insane").

Teach and use the appropriate words for sexual organs and acts.

If a parent discovers his or her daughter when she is engaged in sexual exploration, a parent should not make the daughter feel ashamed of what she is doing.

Do not make inappropriate, leering, or derogatory remarks about other people's bodies.

Do not engage in inappropriate sexual conduct with another adult in front of your children. Affection and warmth toward your partner is nice—extended French-kissing or seductive stroking is not.

Dress appropriate for your age. A forty-year-old woman dressing like a twenty-year-old will not look younger, she will look foolish.

Do not wear clothing printed with vulgarities or offensive statements.

Pay attention to the television shows and movies your daughter is watching, and also the music she is listening to. Flip through the magazines she is reading; even ones targeted to young teens can have content far more mature than you—or she—are comfortable with.

TRY THIS AT HOME

There are many resources available to help parents navigate the tricky waters of human anatomy and sex education. The mothers in my daughter's Brownie troop invited a female ob-gyn whom several of us knew— and who had delivered some of our daughters—to a meeting at the troop leader's home to talk to our girls about their bodies and reproduction. The presentation included anatomically correct plastic molds and some frank talk. We stayed in the room so we could hear (and learn) and be able to follow up at home. At first the girls were embarrassed, but because Dr. Blake was so professional and matter-of-fact, their giggles subsided and they asked excellent questions. If your daughter is not in a Brownie troop, you could put together a group of moms and girls, and offer to reimburse an ob-gyn for her time if she would conduct a mini-seminar.

Some Good Advice

As your daughter develops and her body changes, boys will notice. If your daughter is in sixth grade, the sixth-grade boys may not be overt in their observations. If she attends a middle school that includes seventh and eighth graders with rapidly emerging hormones, however, those boys may assume that because her body is developing, she is fair game for sexual overtures. Be sure your daughter knows that she can be vocal in expressing her discomfort when vulgar words are used in her presence, and that it is not amusing or okay for boys to leer at her and her friends. She should report to a teacher or other school official repeated sexual harassment, and any physical encounters that make her uncomfortable. Talk with her frankly about what she should do if she finds herself in a situation where she feels she is in danger.

Chapter Thirteen

TEMPER TEMPER

At some point in your daughter's early years, no matter how agreeable and sweet natured, she is likely to throw a temper tantrum. My daughter threw a temper tantrum once; she was three years old, prime temper-tantrum-throwing time. We were vacationing on the gulf coast of Florida and because our children were so young—three and one—I cooked most of our meals in the condo. On our last night there, I wanted a reprieve from the kitchen, and we decided on dinner at a popular restaurant that was right on the beach. We spent the forty-five-minute wait out on the deck, where Joy played happily in the sand, throwing bits of crackers to the seagulls. Finally, they called our name, and we were seated. Joy was none too happy to be put into a high chair, which she communicated by squirming, fidgeting, and pouting. Harry dozed in the infant carrier. We ordered, and

I pulled out Joy's coloring book and crayons so she could pass the time as she waited on her fish sticks and fries. After ten minutes she told me she had to go potty, so I picked her up and took her to the bathroom where she fiddled around for a while but nothing more. False alarm, I thought, as we headed back to the table. As I tried to deposit her back in the high chair, she exploded. Hurling herself onto the floor, she commenced to throw a fit that registered about a 7.0 on the Richter scale of temper tantrums. Crying, kicking, flailing, and wailing, she made her position clear. So did I. Scooping her up, I told her father to ask the waiter—who was just then arriving with the long-awaited food—to wrap it all up to go, and I would meet him and Harry at the car. On the way back to the condo, I told her how disappointed we were that her behavior had ruined a night out for all of us, and that it would not be tolerated. Fifteen minutes later, we were back at the condo. Joy was put in her pajamas, then in her high chair, where she sat alone at the table with her cold fish sticks while we went out to the balcony and ate our cold grilled amberjack. She never threw another temper tantrum.

On the other hand, there is a child I know who is infamous for loud, public, and embarrassing displays of ill temper, which his parents have consistently met with bribes, cajoling, and futile attempts to make everything right. We have witnessed this behavior on various occasions since he was a toddler. The last one I saw was when he was ten, and the only thing that had changed was the volume and his more knowledgeable use of vulgar language. I no longer include this family on my guest list.

According to child development experts, temper tantrums are a perfectly natural and predictable expression of a child's first surges of independence—for children ages one to three. It's how parents react to these early, immature, and sometimes embarrassing expressions of frustration that may determine how their daughter learns to manage her anger in the future.

While every parent should expect a temper tantrum from their two- or three-year-old, giving in to the child is the worst possible method of quelling the storm. In the short run, giving in may temper the tempest, but eventually it will produce a young adult without the coping skills necessary to navigate life's inevitable setbacks and disappointments.

When a girl under the age of three has a temper tantrum, a parent should remain calm and walk away. If the tantrum takes place in public—as many do—the parent picks up the child and leaves the party, the store, or the restaurant until the little girl calms down. After she regains control, the parent can hold her and let her know that the parent understands the frustrations of being two, but that throwing a fit—as they say in the South—will not result in the desired objective.

A very young child is not punished for what is truly a natural expression, but she shouldn't be appeased either. After three, parents must let their daughter know in no uncertain terms that temper tantrums will not be tolerated. Not only will she not get what she wants, she will be punished—a time-out or banishment to her bedroom for a set period of time. Just as parents help their daughter learn to recite the alphabet, sing a song, and ride a bicycle, parents are also responsible for helping and teaching their daughter how to control her temper, handle her frustrations, and express her anger in a mature and socially acceptable manner.

Forgive the gross generalization, but in my experience I have found that boys are more likely to respond to hurt, denial, and frustration with anger. They are then more likely to express that anger physically and aggressively. A young girl typically dissolves in tears or uses hurtful words when she is angry, hurt, or frustrated. Although sticks and stones will break bones, unkind words and actions are also weapons that will hurt, often in ways that are crueler and have longer-lasting consequences.

A young lady, no matter how upset she is that she did not get the designer-label shoes she wanted, does not respond by telling her parents that she hates the shoes that they can afford to buy her. No matter how affronted she is when a classmate cuts in front of her in the cafeteria line, a young lady does not respond by calling that person fat or stupid. No matter how frustrated she is for missing the shot, a young lady does not blame a teammate. No matter how disappointed she is that another girl was picked to play the princess in the school play, a young lady does not spread rumors about her rival.

The measure of a mature person is how they react to challenging and difficult situations. Every person, young and old, will sometimes engage in impetuous behavior that he or she will later have cause to regret. An apology takes just a moment but hastens forgiveness and has a lasting effect on relationships. If a young lady loses her temper and says something that hurts another, she first allows herself a moment to cool down, then offers a sincere, in-person apology whenever possible. If face-to-face contact is not possible, then a phone call or letter can substitute.

Your Daughter Is Becoming a Young Lady If . . .

She does not express anger, disappointment, or frustration by using bad language or insulting someone.

She does not express anger, disappointment, or frustration by throwing, kicking, hitting, biting, or breaking something.

If she loses her temper, and does any of the above, she apologizes as soon as she has calmed down.

She does not shout to get someone's attention or pout, sulk, or cry to get what she wants.

She never uses words like *fatso, stupid, butthead, idiot, porky, retard,* or *ugly* when addressing another person.

Parent Pointers

Do not respond to a temper tantrum by giving a child what she wants or promising to get her a treat if she stops.

Do not respond to a temper tantrum with a blast of your own.

If your daughter is having a temper tantrum in a public place, remove her from the other people's presence.

Do not react to your daughter's bad behavior with similar bad behavior: do not bite back so she can see how it feels or spank a child as punishment for hitting.

Do your best not to raise your voice in anger to a child.

Do not yell at other people, question their breeding, or demonstrate the universal display of displeasure, especially not in front of your children.

Try not to fight with your spouse in front of the children.

Do not call other people names, even if you think they deserve it.

If you curse or use vulgarities in front of your children, don't be surprised when they begin using the same words.

Do not throw golf clubs, bats, lamps, jewelry, or anything else in anger.

If you lose your temper in front of your child, apologize. If you lose your temper with your child, apologize.

Accept apologies quickly and graciously when they are made to you.

Part of forgiving is forgetting. Once someone apologizes and you accept the apology, it is over. Let it go.

Try This at Home

When I became a mom, I made a conscious effort to stop cursing, but it still happens. Sometimes I'm not even aware of it. My children may overhear me on the telephone or in a conversation with a friend, and they are quick to point out my infraction. We have a "fine" Jar, and every time I use a curse word, I have to put a quarter in it. Similarly, if my children use the words "shut up," or call someone "stupid" (or even worse, use the two together), they are fined as well. Once a year, we use the collected change for a good cause: for buying books or toys for a family shelter or domestic violence center or to adopt a needy family at Christmas. The rule is that you cannot use the money collected from your bad behavior as a reward to yourself.

Some Good Advice

My mother was a stay-at-home mom with five children. When I was nine, the youngest was born. My mother had plenty of opportunities for discipline. I was often the recipient of her fierce attention, but every time she was forced to have words with me, she did it privately. If your child does something that requires stern words, take her aside and deliver them privately. If the infraction is severe enough to require immediate discipline, take your child home or send the other child home first. Do not discipline your child in public. Humiliation is a form of abuse.

Chapter Fourteen

RELIGION, POLITICS, AND SANTA CLAUS

*T*he cardinal rule of etiquette when it comes to hosting or attending convivial social gatherings is never to bring up religion or politics. That may be true, but if you ask me, it could make for a pretty dull affair. Surely, mature adults can be counted upon to engage in thoughtful discourse on stimulating and controversial topics with respect and regard for opinions that differ from their own. Sadly, that is not always the case.

The exchange of different ideas and philosophies can be stimulating and provocative as long as other viewpoints are not disparaged or vilified. Respect and appreciation for all kinds of people and ideas begins at an early age. Children should be taught to respect the opinions of others no matter how different they may be from their own. This means not ridiculing or making fun of people because of their opinions or beliefs. If someone uses a word or expresses an opinion that is blatantly racist, sexist, vulgar, or otherwise offensive, it is appropriate to end that stream of conversation as quickly as possible.

Until she enters her teens, the strongest influence on a girl will be her parents. As my daughter has gotten older, she overhears discussions among my friends or hears things on the news or from her friends. When my daughter asks me, "What is abortion?" "What is capital punishment?" "What is sexual harassment?" "What is prostitution?" "What is global warming?" I try my best to answer in a factual, objective way. If she asks what I think about the subject, which she usually does, I tell her what I believe and why I believe it, but I also try to objectively present the opposite viewpoint. As she gets older and has more experience, she will form her own opinions, but opinions without knowledge and education stand on pretty shaky ground.

There are many opportunities for parents to teach their daughter respect for different ideologies and beliefs. A young lady might, for example, ask her new friend where he or she attends church, but she does not ridicule her friend for having a different religious affiliation or no affiliation at all.

A young lady can invite a friend to attend church or temple with her. She does not insist that her friend participate in any part of the service that makes him or her uncomfortable. Likewise, a young lady attending services with a friend of a different religious persuasion takes the opportunity to expand her horizons and is respectful of the service and customs, but she is not required to fully participate.

In situations where a public prayer is said, a young lady who does not subscribe to the theology of the assembled does not make a display of her differences but shows respect by remaining quiet through the prayer. If grace is said before a meal where she is a guest, she does not announce that her family does not say grace but simply bows her head.

Political campaigns can offer many teachable moments in fairness, civic responsibility, and respect for people of differing opinions and stances. In recent years, we have unfortunately also had too many moments of shouting, name-calling, and outright lying from every side of the political spectrum. Adults should know better, and should set better examples for children. But when they don't, parents can point out how unproductive such behavior is.

Unless someone is wearing a T-shirt, hat, or pin that announces his or her candidate, a young lady does not ask someone for whom he or she is voting. A young lady does not mock another child's choice or make disparaging comments about his or her candidate.

If a girl holds strong beliefs about a subject—boy bands, the New York Yankees, clothing trends, global warming, or capital punishment—she does not try to impose her beliefs on others, nor does she make fun of or pass judgment on those whose beliefs differ from her own. She may express her thoughts on the topic if she can do so in a courteous and nonconfrontational manner.

When a young lady discovers or is told the truth about Santa Claus, the Tooth Fairy, and the Easter Bunny, she should not expose the myth to other children who may still be captivated by their magic. Once the jig is up on one, it raises some questions about the others. My daughter was snooping around on my dresser one day and discovered the small box where I kept the teeth that the Tooth Fairy had allegedly taken away. I was able to allay her questions with the explanation that the Tooth Fairy brought back the first few teeth so mothers could have them forever. She was skeptical, but went along with it for about another year. Once she decided the Tooth Fairy was bogus, the others followed suit, with Santa being the last to fall. As much as she wanted to show off her inside information, she showed generosity and kindness by keeping the magic alive for her little brother another two years.

Your Daughter Is Becoming a Young Lady If . . .

She does not make fun of or pass judgment on another person's religious beliefs or practices.

She is respectful when attending a religious service with a friend of a different theology.

She does not ask a person for whom they are voting, or for whom they already voted.

She does not make fun of another person's political affiliation.

She does not impose her spiritual or political beliefs on others.

Parent Pointers

Show respect for others' spiritual and political beliefs and do not make or pass judgment in front of your children about another's spiritual or political beliefs.

Do not make a guest in your home or place of worship engage in practices that are uncomfortable to him or her.

Do not say horrid or hateful things about politicians or community leaders, or gossip about them.

Do not call elected officials names; whether you voted for the president of the United States or not, he (or one day she) is still the president of the country and the office is deserving of respect.

TRY THIS AT HOME

If you are of the Christian faith and have friends of the Jewish faith, expose your children to one another's theology by inviting the other family to share in one of your celebrations or religious occasions. Every year we attend one night of Hanukkah at a friend's house and watch the lighting of the menorah and play the dreidel game. We invite them over for a Sunday dinner during Advent, and they participate in lighting the Advent wreath.

Some Good Advice

Talk radio has become increasingly rancorous and acrimonious, with loud, agitated hosts doing their best to provoke angry, venomous, and hostile comments from their callers, which in turn provoke more anger and hostility. This is true of programs dedicated to politics, culture, religion, and sports. The dialogues are often studded with vulgarities and slurs—from both sides of the fence—and there is rarely measured, objective, or thoughtful discourse. These are not appropriate programs for children; if you are a fan of talk radio, do not tune in when children are confined in your car, and be aware of their presence if you are listening at home.

Chapter Fifteen

TELEPHONE MANNERS

I have a friend with three daughters ranging from five to fifteen years old. Every time I call her house, all three girls simultaneously answer on the first ring. I ask to speak with my friend, and I hear a little sigh from each, disappointed that the call wasn't for one of them.

When we first got our two cats, they didn't always use their litter box. I asked my veterinarian what to do about the cats stinking up the house. He asked me how many litter boxes I had; I told him I had one. "Uh-oh," he replied. "In a multi-cat home, you must provide one more litter box than you have cats." No way was I going to have three litter boxes in my laundry room. I got one more, and it alleviated the problem.

If you have more than one girl in your house, you may be tempted to apply the litter box principle to the telephone. As aggravating as it can be, it would be better to teach your girls good telephone manners on the phones already in the home.

Landline use is down dramatically since cell phones have become more affordable and many young singles and couples don't even have one in their home, much less multiple lines. But the generation who was raised on phones attached to a wall with a cord prefers to stay connected in that fashion. One common landline is also efficient for families with children, even when both parents have separate mobile devices. So it behooves young ladies to learn the proper way to use a conventional phone. The telephone may be the most efficient way to reach out and touch someone, but it is also one of modern times' most irritatingly misused forms of communication.

With the exception of knowing how, when, and why to dial 911, a young girl should not be permitted to use the phone until she knows how to do it properly. It is irritating to the caller to have someone answer the phone who doesn't speak clearly or understand what's being said. Before using a phone, your daughter should be articulate enough that she can be understood, and she should be able to accurately take a message.

When she is ready to do so, a young lady answers the telephone in her own home one of the following ways: "Hello" or "Hello, Ray residence, Lauren speaking" or "Ray residence, this is Lauren." She waits for the caller to make the next move. Hopefully, the caller knows telephone manners and will then say,

"Hello Lauren, this is Ms. West, may I speak with your mother, please?" Depending on the circumstances, Lauren would either say, "I'm sorry, she isn't available right now. May I take a message?" or "Just a moment, please." She would then—this is *very* important—either put the receiver down and get her mother or cover the receiver with her hand and call her mother to the phone. She does not yell "Mom" into the telephone.

If her mother and father are not at home, she does not announce the absence of an adult. Instead, she says her mother is not able to come to the phone, and offers to take a message; there should always be a pad of paper and pen next to the phone. A young lady takes the caller's name and number, writing legibly on the pad.

When a young lady places a call from her home phone, she should speak clearly and loudly enough to be heard: "Hello, this is Lauren. May I speak to Caroline, please?" If Caroline is not available or not at home, a young lady then says, "Would you please ask her to call Lauren? My number is 234-5678. Thank you."

A young lady is prepared to leave a recorded message, as nearly every phone, whatever the type; is equipped with voice mail. When a phone is answered by machine or voice mail, a young lady speaks clearly, audibly, and slowly. She does not giggle into the telephone. She makes the message short. "Hello, this is Lauren. Could Caroline call me back at 234-5678? Thank you."

On the subject of answering machines, unless your child can articulate the greeting on your answering machine, leave it to an adult or a computer. If your child can clearly say something like, "This is 798-1700. Please leave a message," then she is ready to record the outgoing announcement.

If a home phone is equipped with call-waiting, a young lady knows how to operate it. If she is on the phone when another call beeps in, she defers to the incoming call, lest it be her mother's boss calling to tell her that she will be fired unless the presentation is ready by noon tomorrow. When another call interrupts her, a young lady takes the next call. If it is for one of her parents, she asks the incoming caller to hold for a moment, goes back to the first call, and asks if she might call back.

Young girls can develop a ferocious attachment to the telephone, but it would be extremely rude of her to monopolize the home's only common landline. Resolve this by setting time limits on the length of her calls, as well as a limit on the number of calls she can make and receive in one day.

A young lady does not place phone calls during inconvenient times, such as the dinner hour, roughly 5:30–7:00 p.m. She does not call a home before 8:00 a.m. or after 9:00 p.m. on weekdays or before 10:00 a.m. or after 10:00 p.m. on weekends. She particularly does not make repeated phone calls to the same house or place calls with no particular reason or purpose in mind.

If a young lady inadvertently dials a wrong number, she does not hang up on recognizing that fact, but instead she says, "I'm sorry, I must have dialed a wrong number." If she is not sure, a young lady asks, "Is this 234-5678?" She does not ask the person answering the phone what number she has called, and if the reverse occurs, she does not give out her telephone number to someone she doesn't know.

A young lady knows that cell phones, no matter how cute, are not toys. Unless she has been given permission to do so, a young lady does not place calls on her parent's cell phone. She does not give her parent's cell phone number to her pals.

Every family makes their own decision based on individual needs and situations regarding what age is the right age for their daughter to have her own cell phone. For some parents, twelve is the magic number, or seventh grade. For others—perhaps both parents have full-time jobs and want their child to be able to reach them instantly if need be—fifth grade might be the right age. Whatever age it is, the first phone can be the most basic of models, capable only of placing and receiving calls, and not equipped for taking photos, texting, or playing games.

Your Daughter Is Becoming a Young Lady If . . .

She speaks clearly and audibly on the telephone.

She does not yell directly into the receiver when calling her mother to the phone.

She knows how to take and leave a message.

She does not call too early in the morning or too late at night.

She does not monopolize the telephone, nor does she place repeated calls to a friend's house, annoying her friend's parents and tying up their phone.

She does not chomp gum or food while on the phone.

She says excuse me if she coughs, sneezes, or belches into the receiver.

She does not take a phone into the bathroom with her.

She does not disregard the call-waiting feature, nor does she forget the original caller.

She returns the portable phone to its receiver.

She does not place long-distance calls without permission from her parents.

She does not answer the phone in someone else's house.

She does not place a call from someone else's house without permission.

She never calls 911 without just cause.

She does not use her cell phone in a movie theater, at the table, or in school.

She does not text incessantly with someone while in the presence of actual people, whether that person is a friend or a parent.

She does not walk and text.

Parent Pointers

Teach your daughter how, when, and why to use 911. Give her some examples of the differences between a real emergency (the house across the street is on fire) and a non-emergency (the cat is up the tree and can't get down).

Make sure your daughter knows her home phone number and her parents' cell numbers and when it is appropriate to share them.

Teach your daughter how to use telephone amenities such as call-waiting and voice mail or answering machines.

Do not chew gum or food while on the phone.

Do not ask your daughter to lie on your behalf, telling a caller you are not available when you simply do not want to take the call.

Do not be rude to telephone solicitors, but cut them off promptly and politely and ask to have your name removed from their calling list.

Turn your cell phone ringer off in public places; if you must make or take a call, excuse yourself and converse privately.

Do not drive and talk on the cell phone simultaneously; it is dangerous, and in an increasing number of states, it is illegal.

Do not drive and text; the consequences of distracted driving can be fatal.

Do not text and walk lest you find yourself walking into a tree or taking a nasty fall.

TRY THIS AT HOME

I don't believe young children need their own phone line. Thanks to cordless phones, a girl can easily find privacy these days. For her eleventh birthday, my daughter received a cordless phone in her bedroom; it shared the family landline, but she felt as if she had her own phone. I did enforce a fifteen-minute restriction on each call, and she wasn't allowed more than one hour a day on the phone.

Some Good Advice

When a girl gets her first cell phone—at whatever age a parent decides is right for their family—perhaps the use is restricted to communication with her family and two best friends. As she gets older and uses her phone responsibly, she can add more friends to her personal directory. Parents should monitor who is in their daughter's directory and call list, and ask questions if they see an unfamiliar name or number. I made my daughter give me her cell phone every night when she went to bed, otherwise I suspect she would have stayed up all night talking and texting.

Chapter Sixteen

COMPUTERS, THE INTERNET, AND SOCIAL MEDIA

*M*y kids are fascinated by photos of me that go way back to before they were born, astonished to find that I had a life before I became their mom. They laugh at the clothes and the hairstyles, and marvel, "Mommy, you look so young!"

One afternoon they were looking through photos taken when I was very, very young—just starting out in my career and working as an assistant editor at a magazine in New York. There I am, in my very first office, sitting at my desk. The surface was strewn with piles of papers, magazines, manuscripts, a vase with a few stalks of eucalyptus (to cut through the cigarette smell prevalent in journalism in those days), a cardboard coffee cup (pre-Styrofoam), and a telephone. Joy was closely studying the photograph, and I was certain she was going to compliment my outfit, or once again exclaim, "Mommy! You look so young!" Instead, she looked at me quizzically and asked, "Mommy, where's your computer?"

I pointed to the small table against the wall beside my desk. "See that thing, Joy? That's a typewriter. It's what we wrote on before computers." Or tried to write on. I was a speedy typist, but not very accurate, and used to joke that the only thing that stood between me and unemployment was a bottle of Wite-Out. I went through that correcting fluid by the case.

Today the delete button is instantaneous, but not necessarily permanent. Technology changes in the blink of an eye, but something young ladies must be taught from the start, is that nothing disappears for good in cyberspace. That questionable photo, that unkind remark, that unsubstantiated rumor, that search through inappropriate material? No matter how many times you hit the delete button, everything remains somewhere out there.

Computer use begins well before preschool, and even pre-readers develop skills that put their parents, and certainly their grandparents, to shame. Having and knowing how to operate a computer or mobile operating system opens the door to a vast universe of information and communication, but it can also be the window to a world of trouble.

Because I work at home and my computer is a crucial tool to my livelihood, my desktop computer has always been off-limits to my children. The family computer—one that I had traded up from—is the one they use and it is on a table in a common room where I can keep an eye on them.

There are many available options in parental control software, easily researched online, with various levels of monitoring. These are strongly recommended installations for the computer your daughter will be using. Schools use control software as well to prevent students from going to inappropriate or unsafe sites.

As your daughter gets older, and proves to be a responsible user, her access can be expanded.

But even the most stringent control systems can be circumvented, and supervision isn't necessarily as strict in other homes as it is in your own. Parental control software does not absolve parents of the task of explaining responsible use of computers, the Internet, and social media to their children. In today's world, it is as important as "the talk" about the birds and the bees.

Not as crucial to their safety, but important to know, is the etiquette of computers and social media.

Young ladies don't monopolize the family computer or use the keyboard after eating glazed donuts without washing their hands first. Young ladies don't place a beverage beside the keyboard unless it has a lid of some type on it. Young ladies know that electronics represent a sizable investment and are careful when using them. Young ladies don't use someone else's computer or laptop without permission.

When young ladies start school and make friends, it is natural that they will want to communicate with them outside of school. Back in the days of typewriters, that was done on the family telephone. Now there are many options available, though it is up to parents which of those their daughter can access and when is the right age.

Prior to getting an e-mail account, a cell phone, and her own Facebook page, my daughter and her friends used AIM to chat on the computer. Watching her fingers fly over the keyboard as she navigated multiple electronic conversations made me dizzy. Now text applications can be used to exchange messages via iPods. Google's Buzz networking and messaging tool is another option young girls with a gmail address can use pre–Facebook access. There are also social network sites that have been created to provide communication exclusively between family members and family friends that might be a safe entry point for young children to social networks, but as with anything, parents should thoroughly research the sites.

Increasingly, schools and teachers are using e-mail to communicate everything from homework assignments, test scores, grades, and schedule changes. The grade level at which students are included in that communication is up to the particular school your daughter attends, but typically, public schools lag behind private schools in the use of technology.

Assist your daughter in setting up her first e-mail account, even if she can run circles around you when it comes to tech savvy. Make sure her e-mail address is appropriate and does not unintentionally give out too much information. There is extensive assistance available online to guide parents in assuring their daughters' online safety and not compromise her personal information or that of your family. Identity theft is common and a nightmare to resolve.

Facebook was originally intended as a networking and social site for college students, and in order to set up a page, members had to have an authentic college e-mail address. That is no longer true, and everyone from your twelve-year-old babysitter to your eighty-two-year-old grandmother can have a Facebook page.

For my daughter, I decided that the start of seventh grade was the time she could become a Facebook member and have her own e-mail address. The key word is *watch*. Be certain your daughter understands that you will be monitoring her buddy lists, her address book, and her "friends" on Facebook. Make certain she uses the highest level privacy setting and allows communication only with friends on her own list.

In no uncertain terms, explain to your daughter that saying hurtful or mean things, and sending or posting inappropriate photos is wrong, and while it may only take one second to do it, it can't be taken back. A good standard for her to keep in mind is that she should not say anything online that she would not say to someone's face, and should not send a photo that she would have to hide from her parents or be ashamed if they saw it.

No doubt, as I type these words, the next big thing is being developed and will replace all the previous "next big things." But the central message remains the same. It is crucial that you stay aware, informed, educated, and engaged enough to keep your daughter safe. That does not mean reading every message she receives, just as you wouldn't open every piece of mail addressed to her. It does mean knowing the password to her accounts, and requiring her to accept you as a "friend," if only until you are confident that she understands the dangers that can lurk in shadows of the big world online.

Your Daughter Is Becoming a Young Lady If . . .

She stops what she is doing on the computer when her mother calls her for dinner or her father asks her to let the dog out.

She does not text while she is interacting with people in her presence.

She does not try to circumvent the restrictions her parents place on her computer usage.

She does not say something online that she would not say to someone's face.

She does not send or post unflattering photos of others, nor does she send inappropriate photos of herself to anyone for any reason.

She does not go to sites marked "For Adults Only."

She does not go to unprotected chat rooms.

She does not accept friend requests from people she doesn't know.

She does not divulge personal information about herself or her family over the Internet or social networks.

Parent Pointers

Keep the family computer in a common room, where you can monitor when and how your daughter uses it.

Insist your daughter gives you her password for any computer and social network accounts she has.

Do not read her mail or listen to her voice mail messages. Monitoring her use of the computer and social networks is a wise precaution for her safety; electronic eavesdropping and policing is invasive and counterproductive.

Detailed call lists for each cell phone line you are responsible for is available online. Check your daughter's list and know which numbers are in her network of friends. If anything raises a red flag, ask her about it; don't jump to conclusions and blast her.

Do not text, check your e-mails, take or make calls while your daughter is talking to you, or when you are in the stands at her game or the audience of her recital. Your child should not feel she is competing for your attention with your mobile device.

TRY THIS AT HOME

In addition to blocking access to certain sites, parents can also set limits on the hours their daughter can access the Internet, and for how long—for example, one hour per day, and not after 9:00 p.m. Leave it up to your daughter how she wants to use that time. Joy would typically spend thirty minutes after school messaging with her friends, and then her other thirty minutes just before cut-off time. She made "dates" to talk to her friends during her accessible hours.

Some Good Advice

Deciding what is the right age for a girl to get a cell phone, access to a messaging site, a Facebook page, and more access to social media is an individual family decision. It can be difficult if your daughter's best friend has access to Google Buzz but your daughter does not, or if all her friends except her have cell phones and are texting, and she is being held hostage by the family phone landline. When your daughter is young, you probably have some type of relationship with her friends' parents, fostered by car pools, soccer teams, classroom volunteering, birthday parties and sleepovers. Discuss with the other parents what their thoughts are. If you can come to a common agreement—for example, computer access in fifth grade, cell phones in seventh, and Facebook pages in high school—it will be easier on everyone.

Chapter Seventeen

STARING AND DIFFERENCES

*D*rive down any main artery or visit any mall in any village, town, or city in America, and you will see the exact same stores and restaurants: Gap, Old Navy, Target, Walgreens, the Limited, Starbucks, Taco Bell, Domino's, TCBY, and Wendy's. We want to know that when we drive from one city to another we will be able to find something familiar: a Wendy's with the same chicken nuggets and the same fries. If we travel five hundred miles from home and need a T-shirt, we can find an Old Navy, walk straight to the girls' department, and find one just like what we forgot and left at home.

Years ago, a friend of mine went with her fiancé and his parents to New Jersey for a college football game. One day they ventured into the big city, but instead of getting out of the car, they drove by everything—they drove by the Empire State Building;

they drove by Central Park; they drove by Rockefeller Center. When it came time to eat, they drove right by the thousands of opportunities to expand their culinary horizons that the most diverse city in the world offers, and instead, they drove back to New Jersey, directly to a McDonald's.

Whether it's food, culture, music, the arts, or people, parents do their children no favors by insulating them from the world. Sooner or later most children will venture out beyond the four corners of the world they grew up in, and it will help them immeasurably to have had exposure to and interaction with people who are different from them.

Parents should show their children that bigoted remarks, slurs, and jokes will not be tolerated in their presence. One need not become incensed or confrontational. Saying something like "We would prefer not to hear those kinds of remarks" or "We don't find that funny" should be enough to get your message across.

Aside from meeting people whose skin color, ethnic background, sexual orientation, or socio-economic status differs from their own, children will also meet people who are different from them because of physical or mental handicaps, or disfigurement due to disease or accidents. Small girls can be forgiven for staring and asking awkward questions: "Why is that man in a wheelchair?" "What's on that lady's face?" "Why can't that boy talk?"

Parents first tell their daughter that she does not

stare or, even worse, point at people different from her, but that she may quietly ask her parent a question about people in a wheelchair or with a horrid scar on their face or with a developmental handicap. The parent explains that perhaps the person has had an accident that put him in a wheelchair or that she may have suffered a terrible burn or that sometimes things happen before babies are born and not everyone turns out the same as everyone else.

A young lady treats handicapped children she may meet as she would anyone else. A young lady should always ask before assisting. If she meets a man who is deaf, a young lady gets his attention by lightly touching his arm or shoulder. A young lady does not shout at a deaf person, but speaks distinctly, not rushing her words. Many deaf people have been taught to read lips, so a young lady should be certain her mouth is clearly visible and that she speaks articulately.

If a young lady meets a woman who is blind, there is no need to help her move about unless asked. A young lady makes her arrival or departure known verbally to a blind person. If a blind person has a guide dog, a young lady does not pet the dog without permission, nor does she throw a ball, ask him to do tricks, or try to feed him a snack; the dog is his master's eyes, and to take him away from his job could be harmful.

When speaking to a person in a wheelchair, a young lady makes every effort to have that conversation at eye level so that the person in the wheelchair does not get a crick in his or her neck. She does not try to assist the person in the wheelchair unless she is asked.

Mentally challenged children and grown-ups can be frightening to children, so parents should make every effort to explain the illness or disability to their daughter and assure her that there is nothing to be afraid of. A young lady treats a mentally challenged person with compassion, respect, and patience.

Your Daughter Is Becoming a Young Lady If . . .

She does not judge a book by its cover or a person by the color of his or her skin, religion, clothing, house, car, or lifestyle.

She does not ask blunt questions like, "Are you rich?" "Are you poor?" "Are you mentally challenged?"

She does not engage in name-calling or jokes that disparage someone different from her.

She does not stare or point at people with handicaps, disabilities, or physical defects.

She does not shout at physically disabled or mentally challenged people in an effort to be understood.

She does not act as if a handicap makes a person invisible, a blind person deaf, or a deaf person stupid.

She shows kindness, respect, and patience for the handicapped and challenged.

Parent Pointers

Never make racial or ethnic slurs.

Do not repeat racist, sexist, or ethnic jokes or tolerate them in your presence.

Do not stare at or whisper about the handicapped.

Never park in a handicapped space, not even for a minute, unless you are physically in need of the spot and have the authorization to use it.

Answer as simply as possible your daughter's questions about people different from her.

Try This at Home

If you know people who are handicapped in some way, and they are agreeable, ask them to talk to your daughter about their handicap, explaining how it happened, how they overcame it, how they live with it every day, and what others do that hurts them and helps them. Knowing a person with a handicap makes all the difference in the world and goes a long way toward satisfying natural curiosity and allaying fears.

Some Good Advice

Exposing your daughter to people of different skin colors, religions, ethnic backgrounds, or sexual preferences gives her the opportunity for hands-on lessons in understanding, respect, and tolerance. If everyone in your neighborhood, your place of worship, or the school your daughter attends looks just like you, you may have to make an effort to introduce your daughter to people different from yourselves. Many cities have events like a culture day that bring people of different ethnic backgrounds together. If you live in a suburb, consider volunteering once a week at an inner-city community center or an outreach program.

Chapter Eighteen

PREACHERS AND TEACHERS; CHURCH AND SCHOOL

*A*t whatever age and stage your little girl enters the arena of professional childcare and formal education—day care, preschool, or kindergarten—she is bound to have some fears and anxiety. If you want your daughter to adjust to this important milestone in her development, you will just have to buck up when she is wailing as if her heart were breaking as you walk out the door. Chances are she will be happily engaged in play ten minutes later, while you are sitting in your car wailing as if your heart will break.

Even if your daughter has been in day care and is accustomed to being away from her parents for much of the day, the first day of kindergarten can provoke nervousness about the new school, new teachers, and new friends. Most schools recognize this and plan some type of orientation where the principal introduces herself, the kindergarten teachers, the school secretaries, and the librarian.

If your school does not offer this—or even if it does—it is helpful to take a trip to the school with your daughter a day or two before school starts. The teachers are readying their classrooms, hanging up decorations, and getting their supplies in order. Drop by just long enough to introduce yourself and your daughter, take a quick peek at the room, walk around the halls, stop into the office to say hello to the principal and secretaries; you may even bring some fresh flowers for the teacher and a plate of brownies for the office staff. When your daughter comes to school the first day, there are familiar, friendly faces awaiting her, and she already feels comfortable in the classroom. The preschool visit is something I continued through elementary school.

Parents can familiarize their daughter with general school rules before she begins—the teacher is the boss, no talking out of turn, raise your hand, pay attention—and the teacher will no doubt add some of his or her own. Most elementary schools also hold an open house soon after school begins; parents should make every effort to attend this as teachers describe a typical day, their individual teaching styles, and their rules and expectations.

Once she begins school, a young lady should know that the classroom is the teacher's domain, and unless she is asked to do something that goes against her religion or customs of her people, she follows the laws of the land.

A young lady does nothing to disturb the teacher or peers. She completes her assignments from the evening before and is prepared every morning with the necessary school supplies. She sits in her seat and does not invade the physical space of her classmates, nor does she take any of their supplies without permission. She does not talk while the teacher is teaching or while others are working. She does not whisper secrets or pass notes to her friends. She never copies from a classmate's paper. In the cafeteria, she remembers her table manners and cleans up after herself. She does not take food from another child, make unkind remarks about another child's food or eating habits, and never throws food.

On the playground, a young lady waits her turn for the swings and hanging bars and follows rules of play in whatever game her classmates are engaged. If a young lady wears a dress or skirt to school and is active on the playground, she wears a pair of shorts under her dress. A young lady does not exclude others. If another child wishes to join in the game, a young lady either welcomes him or her in or promises to do so when an appropriate pause in the game is reached. If a young lady wants to join a group of classmates already engaged in play, she asks instead of just barging in. She does not try to change a game in process.

In some churches, the first experience a child will have with formal church is her baptism, a sacred moment for family and friends. The precious baby girl dons something fancy, often an heirloom baptismal gown, and has a bow or bonnet on her head. Proudly the parents hand their little angel over to the minister. The entire congregation looks on expectantly. If she is typical of most babies, the moment the water is poured over her head, she will burst into a startled and piercing wail. Everyone smiles indulgently at the darling infant.

It is darling only at that stage. After the baptism, the sound of a squalling infant or rambunctious toddler strikes discord in solemn services. Some churches deal with this issue by providing crying rooms in the back of the church where the parent can retreat with the noisy baby and remain included in the service. Other churches and synagogues provide child care during the service.

A young lady who is permitted to sit with the grown-ups follows the common guidelines of courtesy while she is in church or temple. If she is not old enough to read and follow along with the order of service, a young lady brings along something unobtrusive to keep herself busy. A young girl does not bring along a baby doll with crying and wailing features, the ninety-six-crayon jumbo box, or her portable loom.

A pre-reader can bring a sticker book, a coloring book, or a sketch pad and some markers. She is not expected to do anything other than remain occupied and quiet for the duration. A young lady does not lie down on a pew or on the floor or hang over the back of her pew staring at the people behind her. She can write on the bulletin, but never in a hymnal or prayer book. She does not remove all the printed material from the back of the pews to use as a coloring book or to practice her origami.

Regarding communion or similar sacrament, some churches set an age when children may participate. Catholics, for instance, have a First Communion ceremony that takes place when the child is about six or seven. Other churches allow any baptized person to take communion, and still others require a public profession of faith as a requirement. If your child approaches the communion rail with her thumb plugging her mouth, she is too young to take communion.

When she is old enough to read, a young lady is encouraged to take part in the service; at the very least, standing when the congregation stands, sitting when they sit, and kneeling when they kneel. By the time she is nine or ten years old, a young lady participates in those parts of the service that call for congregation participation: reciting creeds and prayers or singing hymns. If your clergyperson is extremely long-winded, or if your congregation is so large that communion takes more than twenty minutes to conduct, a young lady can engage herself in a book or sketch pad brought along for that purpose.

A young lady treats her clergyperson or religion teacher with respect, using the proper title: Reverend Stevens, Father Francis, Rabbi Kantor. If your clergyperson's habit is to stand in the back of the church following the service to greet his or her parishioners, a young lady stops briefly with her parents and says "hello," shaking hands if the clergyperson initiates the exchange.

Your Daughter Is Becoming
a Young Lady If . . .

She dresses in the fashion of the church or temple she is attending. If jeans are acceptable apparel, she may wear them.

She does not chew gum in school or church.

She does not eat or drink in the chapel or temple.

She does not talk out of turn at school or in religion class.

She does not whisper or giggle in her friends' ears during class or religious services.

She adheres to the dress code of her school.

She addresses clergy and school staff by the appropriate titles.

When she needs to go to the restroom during church, temple, or school, she does not disturb others en route.

She does not linger at the water fountain and keep others waiting in line.

She does not take a posse of girls into the bathroom with her and take up residence, particularly if others are waiting.

Parent Pointers

Get your children to school on time, properly dressed, and prepared with what they need for the day.

Be respectful to your daughter's teacher or administrator.

Let your children know that in the school the faculty and administration are in charge.

If there is a disagreement between your child and teacher or administrator, address it privately with the appropriate school representatives.

Communicate frequently with your child's teachers about your child's behavior in class, regarding play and work.

Do not impose unruly children on fellow congregants.

If your church or temple has a service that is more attuned to children—usually the earlier service—make all efforts to attend that one.

Do supply small girls with something—quiet and discreet—to occupy them during the service.

Dress appropriately for church or temple.

Do not chatter with your spouse, friends, or children during the service.

Pay attention to the service, including the sermon, and do not use the time as an opportunity to pay bills or catch up on correspondence.

Never text in church or temple or check your e-mails on your mobile device.

Sit closer to the front of the church or temple so that your children can see and be more engaged.

Encourage your daughter to participate in the service when she is old enough.

Address the clergy with their proper titles.

Try This at Home

Just before my daughter started kindergarten, all eighty or so children who would be starting that fall were invited to a kindergarten roundup. Four sets of parents hosted a cookout in one very large backyard for the class of 2008 and their families. It gave the kids and the parents the chance to meet one another in a fun, informal setting. Recruit some other parents to help you out. If no one has a backyard large enough, try a park, or even—if the school grants permission— on the school grounds.

Some Good Advice

Many churches have a children's choir. When my daughter was beginning second grade—the earliest entry age at our church—she joined the Choristers, who led the music at the early service every Sunday. Not only did it offer an invaluable education in classical and theological music, it also required her attention to and participation in the service and instilled a mature level of discipline. If your child can't carry a tune, many faiths offer opportunities for children to serve as acolytes; children can also assist a parent who ushers.

Chapter Nineteen

MEAN GIRLS AND BULLYING

The day before fifth grade began—and the first year of lower middle school in our district—my daughter and I went to the school to have a look around and see which teacher she was assigned to. Class lists were posted on a wall outside the office, and Joy scanned them to find her name. In the blink of an eye, I saw her eagerness fade and a wave of anxiety cross her face. I asked her what was wrong and she mumbled, "Nothing, let's go." I quickly looked at the list and saw several names I recognized, including one girl we had both known nearly since birth.

The next morning, dressed in the "first-day-of-school-outfit" she had picked out, she got out of the car and walked reluctantly through the front doors of the school, looking back at me just once. Seven hours later when I came back to pick her up, she was barely in the car before she began sobbing.

The good news: she had been assigned to someone considered the best and most demanding teacher of that grade level at the school. The bad news: so were six girls who had formed a tight, impenetrable clique as far back as kindergarten. Not until this year were they all in the same classroom together, which they celebrated by wearing nearly identical outfits the first day. Joy's new outfit apparently did not pass muster and was obviously whispered and giggled about. She never wore it again.

Joy had a casual friendship with each of them, but she was not a certified member of the "Band of Six." Their exclusionary tactics had apparently been finely honed over the summer, and were implemented almost immediately, carried out in the classroom, lunchroom, and playground, supplemented with snide remarks about other girls' appearances, clothes, taste in music, or athletic performances.

Joy didn't know any of the other girls in the classroom well, and she dreaded every single day. By the end of the first week, I considered asking the principal to move her to another teacher. Instead, Joy and I had a serious talk about alternatives and how to manage the situation so she could take advantage of the great teacher and try to make the proverbial lemonade out of lemons.

I spoke to the teacher, sharing the history, and asked him to keep an eye on the situation in his classroom. He responded the next day with assigned seating, breaking up the girls for at least the hours they spent under his eagle eye. He put Joy in the front of the room, beside a girl he suspected she might become friends with—he was right.

I talked to Joy about avoiding situations that would allow them to exclude her—not to try to sit at their table in the cafeteria or join their members-only basketball game on the playground. I urged her to join a club that allowed her gift as a computer whiz and a writer to shine, and to make new friends with the members of those groups. She emerged as an ace on the kickball team, which included more kids than the mean girls' three-on-three basketball games.

It wasn't an easy year for her, and not for her mother either, because like all parents I would move mountains if it would prevent my child from being hurt. But she made it through, stronger and more self-confident than when she began.

Compared to some horror stories I have heard, the treatment my daughter received was mild, but painful nonetheless.

Parents of daughters should know that while boys' bullying is almost always physical and therefore can be easier to spot, girls primarily bully through social exclusion, or "relational bullying." Those girls aspire to the label "mean girls" and they exist in every school. Even if your daughter is not a victim—or possibly worse, a mean girl herself—parents should educate themselves on the topic, how to recognize it and how to deal with this very real problem. It can begin as young as preschool, and unchecked it can result in serious problems for your daughter in the future, whatever side of the divide she is on.

It can also escalate—as girls get older and have more access to technology—to cyber-bullying, which can take off like a runaway train. Young ladies need to understand that the things they post on Facebook or send via text message, can go viral in an instant and result in serious consequences that can never be undone. If your daughter is the victim of a cyber attack, she will need your help to halt it and stem the damage.

Putting sophisticated technology in the hands of immature adolescents who are subject to strong, irrational emotions and bursts of temper is akin to giving them a loaded weapon without a safety lock. At that age, living in the moment, it is nearly impossible to understand and foresee the damage that can be unleashed with the simple click of a "send" button.

Schools, churches, synagogues, community centers, and civic groups offer seminars for parents and children on this topic, and there is a wealth of information available in books and online. It is imperative that parents educate themselves on the subject, be proactive, and address any hint of a problem with their daughter quickly.

Your Daughter Is Becoming a Young Lady If . . .

She knows that making another person feel small succeeds only in diminishing herself.

She does not giggle or snicker at a classmate's answer to a teacher's question or the classmate's inability to answer a question.

She does not make fun of or remark badly on a classmate's grades on a test or report card.

She does not make fun of a classmate's clothing or fashion sense.

She does not tease others in a way that hurts feelings.

She comes to the defense of a classmate who is being teased or harassed by bullies.

She lets her teacher or parents know and asks for their help if she is the victim of bullies.

She does not form cliques or clubs with the purpose of excluding others, or create groups on Facebook for the purpose of excluding or hurting others.

She does not give out her social network passwords, even to her best friend, and she always logs out of whatever computer she is using.

She does not send mean or hateful messages through texting or social networking, or send or post photos that would hurt another.

Parent Pointers

Educate yourself about social exclusion and relational bullying—its impact, how to recognize it, and how to respond.

Talk to your daughter about what bullying is and how harmful it can be.

If you suspect your daughter is being hurtful or deliberately exclusionary to other girls, address it calmly, but purposefully, and don't stop talking about it until you are sure she understands that it is far from harmless.

Explain to your daughter that if she is being bullied in any way, she should tell you so you can help her handle it.

Be clear that if she has been subjected to any type of cyber attack, she should not respond or engage, as that will only escalate the attack. She should not delete whatever has been sent or posted, but come to her parents immediately and show them, even if what has been posted is embarrassing to her.

If your child has been bullied at school, talk to the teacher and administration and make them aware of the problem. Ask that they speak also to anyone who has contact with the mean girls and their victims, including librarians, cafeteria workers, and playground supervisors. If that doesn't end the bullying, request a meeting at the school with the perpetrator's parents, teachers, and the administration.

If your daughter's school does not offer bullying awareness for students, urge them to do so, beginning with the basics in kindergarten and continuing at every grade level with developmental awareness.

TRY THIS AT HOME

If your daughter is being excluded from a group of girls, talk with her about how to respond. Act out and practice some verbal and nonverbal responses to hurtful comments and actions. Perhaps she can take this opportunity to seek out someone who is new to school, or who has been in a different classroom in previous years. Urge her to find other girls to sit with at lunch, or a group of boys and girls. Take part in a team sport on the playground, or join an after-school club.

Some Good Advice

Despite your best efforts to establish open communication with your daughter, she may be afraid of being labeled a tattletale and not tell you that she is being bullied. Be alert for some telltale signs. Is she dreading school? Does she seem to have no friends? Has she become clingy and prone to tears? If she is being criticized over her weight, she might respond by overeating or by developing an eating disorder. Pay attention to nonverbal signals your daughter is sending you, and have a private, calm, reassuring talk with her. Chances are, if it is happening, she wants to tell you but doesn't know how.

Chapter Twenty

GOOD SPORTSMANSHIP

*I*t's not whether you win or lose, but how you play the game." Every young lady should be taught the axiom before she knows how to hold a tennis racquet or pick up a baton. Long before your daughter sets foot on a soccer field or joins a debate club, she will have opportunities to practice good sportsmanship. Is there a home in America with small children that doesn't own a game of *Candyland*? The route to the top of Candy Mountain can be a girl's first lesson in winning and losing. She will no doubt be disappointed if, just as she is preparing to summit, the luck of the draw sends her all the way back to Gumdrop Village. Do not be tempted to allow her to draw again for a better card. The only way a child can learn to be a good loser is by losing, and then seeing that it is not the end of the world. Besides, the eventual successful ascending of Candy Mountain will be all the sweeter when achieved fairly.

Though sportsmanlike conduct is typically associated with sporting events, it is integral to every contest, from tennis matches and hockey games to beauty pageants and auditions. Still, there is something about the decorum and environment of a spelling bee—which offers incredibly intense competition—that does not lend itself to kicking the podium or hitting the victor if one misses the final word.

Some of the most blatant exhibitions of bad sportsmanship ever witnessed have taken place not in professional sports, but at little league games, and not from children but from their parents.

When my daughter was ten, she began playing softball in a very competitive league. Most of the parents sat together somewhere in the vicinity of the dugout, but one mother sat off by herself. After a couple of games, we were glad she did. Every time her daughter came to bat, or had a fielding chance, this mother yelled. If her daughter did well, she cheered as if she had just won the league championship single-handedly. But if she failed, the mother would berate and chastise her daughter loudly enough that everyone on both teams could hear. If the umpire made a call against her, the mother was on her feet vigorously protesting. It was humiliating and usually left the child in tears. The coach spoke to the mother several times, but it did no good. Midway through the season, the girl quit. The incident was a reminder to us all to watch our own behavior.

When I was growing up, there were precious few opportunities for girls to participate in sports, in or out of school. Thankfully, that has changed, and my daughter is engaged in as many sports as my son. Though it would be terrific if she were awarded an athletic scholarship to college, we emphasize that games are meant, first and foremost, to be fun, and when it stops being fun, what's the point? Putting pressure on a child to win, or to please an overbearing or overly engaged parent, only contributes to an atmosphere that is fertile for bad behavior.

Once your daughter is signed up for a sport, a parent relinquishes game-time authority to the coach, unless it is clear that a coach is exhibiting poor sportsmanship. When playing in a team sport, a young lady acknowledges her coach's authority and sublimates her individual aspirations for the common goal of the team.

A coach is charged with teaching the rules of the game and good manners during the competition. Besides accurate aim or quick feet, there are more intangible tools a young lady brings to the game. A young lady has a positive, generous attitude, always aware that a team sport requires teamwork. She doesn't hog the ball but passes if her teammate is in a better position to score. If she misses the shot or strikes out, she can show that she is disappointed but does not stomp her feet, kick the goal post, throw the bat, or toss her batting helmet. In most sports, unseemly shows of temper are enough to get a player ejected from the game. If your daughter's behavior merits such an ejection, consider it a wake-up call for both of you. Do not question or chastise the umpire or referee; instead, have a long and private talk with your daughter and her coach when tempers have cooled.

A young lady doesn't question or argue the decisions of the coach or the call of the umpire or referee. She does not roll her eyes, make disrespectful faces, or mutter disdainful comments under her breath at those calls or decisions. When it is time for the sides to change or play to resume, she hustles and does not hold up the game. A young lady does not offer excuses for a mistake or bad play—"the sun was in my eyes" or "I had a crick in my neck"—but apologizes to her teammates for any lapse that may have hurt the team. Teammates should accept her apology without recrimination. A young lady does not make fun of a mistake or failure of a member of the opposing team.

In most children's sports, after the game is concluded, both sides line up and shake hands or exchange hand slaps with the opposing players. A young lady participates in this ritual with sincerity, without grumpiness or boasting, remembering that being a gracious winner is as important as being a good loser.

The rules of good sportsmanship apply to any competition, whether it is organized sports or playground kickball, a casual challenge tossed from one girl to another to race across the swimming pool or a crucial swim meet, a spelling bee or a chess match. Be fair, be generous, be accommodating, be flexible, and be willing to compromise. Without those principles of fair play, no one wins.

Your Daughter Is Becoming
a Young Lady If . . .

She does not gloat over a win or sulk over a loss.

She does not accuse another player of cheating, even if she knows it to be true.

She knows the rules of play but is willing to admit when she is wrong.

She yields to the authority of her coach and referees.

She does not cross the line between aggressive play and assault.

She stays engaged in the game, on the field or from the bench.

She does not make fun of another player's mistakes, even players on opposing teams.

She commends the efforts of a teammate, even if the effort fails.

She acts as a booster for her teammates.

She congratulates the winner if she loses, and thanks the other team or her opponent for a good game if she wins.

Parent Pointers

Do not "let" your children win a game.

Remind your daughter that games are meant to be fun, and if her conduct is making it less so, she cannot play.

Remind your daughter to include everyone who wants to play in the game, even if one child's ability is not commensurate with her teammates.

Learn yourself and then teach your daughter the rules and courtesies of the sport in which she is participating.

Yield to the authority of coaches and referees. If they need your advice, opinion, or help, they will ask.

Do not facilitate or enable your daughter's whining about something not being "fair." Remind her that just because something did not go her way doesn't mean that it's not fair.

Do not do anything to embarrass your daughter, whether cursing at the umpire or calling her by a private family nickname when she comes to bat.

Resist the urge—this is particularly true for mothers—to run onto the field or court and check your child's injury. This is the coach's job.

Resist the urge—this is particularly true for fathers—to usurp the coach's game plan or question his or her decisions.

Never berate, yell, or curse at your daughter, her teammates, opposing players, opposing coaches, opposing parents, or officials; never throw or hit things in disappointment or disgust.

Act as every child's booster, not just your own. This includes commending a particularly exceptional play by an opposing player.

Congratulate the winners if you lose; commend the losers for a good effort.

When you are the visiting team, remember you are a guest, and act as you would if you were in their home. Clean up your area in the stands before you leave.

Try This at Home

I abhor the playground practice of "picking" teams, particularly if everyone is obligated to play and cannot opt out for another activity. One by one, the best players are chosen, as the lesser ones shrink slowly, until finally only two remain, thoroughly humiliated, dreading the next selection that will reveal which of the two is the least wanted child. I am not an advocate of finding every inane opportunity to boost a child's self-esteem, but being the last one picked is a confidence destroyer. There are better ways to do it, and parents, teachers, and PE instructors should make sure they are used. Here's one: Place the children in a straight line and have them count off one, two, three, four—all the ones and threes on one side, all the twos and fours on the other. Allowing children to pick the best players first in order to stack a team belies the lesson that it's just a game.

SOME GOOD ADVICE

Do not force your daughter to play a sport she doesn't want to play, even if she has a superior talent for it. My daughter is very athletic, and since she was five years old, she has played soccer in the spring and fall, and basketball in the winter. One spring she was recruited by a coach to play for his team in a local girls' softball league, so she gave up soccer that season to try softball. Even before official play began, the other girls and parents were amazed at how quickly she picked up the game. Because she was one of the stronger girls on the team, she was positioned as catcher; she was also the only girl on the team who could handle the fast pitch. Though she quickly became known as one of the better catchers in the league, she was clearly not having fun. Joy likes to run—thus her propensity for soccer and basketball—and was bored crouching behind home plate for the duration of a game. Though the coach implored her to give it another try, she and I decided that there was no reason for her to play a game that did not bring her any pleasure, and she went back to soccer.

Chapter Twenty-one

WRITTEN CORRESPONDENCE

I am fairly certain that I have just about every personal letter and greeting card I have ever received. I still have my one-year-old birthday cards (thanks to my mother, equally sentimental about letters). I still have the letters my entire second-grade class wrote to me when I was in the hospital with pancreatitis, the letters my parents and siblings wrote me when I went to sleep-away camp the first time, the letter my father wrote me when I left home at nineteen, the letters my late grandmother wrote me while I was living in New York, letters from friends, letters from my grown siblings that enclosed the annual school photos of their children, love letters from old boyfriends, and the last letters my aunt wrote me, in a nearly illegible hand, before she died of breast cancer.

My family is a family of letter writers, with everyone keeping track of who "owes" whom a letter. My mother sends out a calendar every year with everyone's birthday and anniversary, and periodic updates as a new baby is born or a new girlfriend enters the picture. Woe be unto those who neglect to send at least a postcard to observe the milestone.

Since my entire family became connected to the Internet, we e-mail each other at least weekly. Sometimes the e-mail is directed to just one recipient; sometimes it is sent to everyone. While it is great to have that instant communication, it has meant a dramatic decline in the number of letters that arrive via snail mail. I print out some of the e-mails to save, but it simply is not the same as having a tangible keepsake of your loved ones in the form of their stationery and handwriting; I really miss that.

Even if you are not as obsessive as my family, somewhere—in a special box, in her baby book, in the bottom of a drawer—is tucked away your child's first scribbled communication. Short and sweet, embellished with a heart or a flower or stick figure, these first letters are infinitely endearing in their earnest simplicity.

Written correspondence is one of the greatest, most enduring, and priceless gifts we can offer one another. There is something very special about finding—amid the bills, advertisements, solicitations, appointment reminders, and credit card offers—a handwritten note or letter from an old friend, a far-away relative, or a daughter.

According to standard rules of etiquette, there are three types of letters that should always be handwritten (unless a disability prevents it): notes of condolence, replies to formal invitations, and thank-you notes.

Children will have rare occasion to write condolence notes or formal invitations, but they have plenty of opportunities to write thank-you notes. It is good policy, and may ease the way down the road, to get children into the habit of writing thank-you notes at an early age, even before they are able to write. Make it fun for them and make good use of their imagination. When my children were toddlers, we used finger paints to put their handprints on sheets of paper, then they wrote their names as best they could. I would add a short note of my own. Later, we graduated to drawing pictures of the gift they had received, and finally, worked our way up to writing. Stationery companies make preprinted, fill-in-the-blank thank-you notes for children, but frankly, I'd prefer a paper towel with a Kool-Aid stain and a note in crayon.

Teach your daughter that when someone is thoughtful enough to remember her with a gift for her birthday, Christmas, Hanukkah, or a special ceremony, that gesture must be acknowledged in a personal and prompt fashion (though late is better than never at all). While strict guidelines of etiquette call for a thank-you note to be sent within two or three days of receipt of a gift, we wait and do them all at one time.

Children's thank-you notes can be written on almost anything at all, but providing a box of children's stationery—usually ruled and imprinted with her first name—that she chooses herself can make the endeavor more enjoyable.

More than any other type of correspondence, thank-you notes can be written in a conversational style, which is the way most children naturally write anyway. A young lady begins her thank-you note with the appropriate salutation: "Dear Grandma," "Dear Uncle Jim and Aunt Katie," "Dear Andrew."

If the gift is from a group of people—an aunt, uncle, and cousins—she can begin: "Dear Aunt Merri, Uncle Ken, Keller, and Coby." If the size of the family makes that salutation too wordy, she can say, "Dear Shaws."

She acknowledges the specific gift with a brief note of what makes it special: "Thank you for the beading kit. I made a necklace for my best friend and one for me." "Thank you for the Little House book. Those are my favorites!"

Little girls' birthday parties are typically frenetic affairs, but it is important that when a young lady opens her presents she keep the accompanying card with the present or opens at such a pace to allow someone to keep a list of the presents and their givers. It is rude to race through a pile of presents.

If she received cash, she makes some mention of how she has used it, or intends to. "Thank you for the check for my confirmation. I used it to buy a new case for my iPod" or "Thank you for the check for my birthday. I am going to use it for spending money on our vacation." In the case of a gift certificate, she can write, "Thank you for the gift certificate to Bath & Body. I love that store and can't wait to go!"

If the gift is from a friend who came to a birthday party, she might add, "Thanks for coming to my party." If the gift is from a relative who lives far away, she might say, "I wish you could have been here for my birthday."

In closing, she can simply say, to a friend, "Thanks again. Joy." To a relative she could say, "Thank you again. Love, Joy." To someone far away, she can write, "I hope to see you soon. Joy."

A young lady who has legible enough handwriting addresses the envelopes and seals and stamps them, saving her parents the trouble. Parents should perform a final inspection for the correct address and postage.

When a girl is nine or ten years old, she is old enough to write and send the invitations to her own birthday parties. These can be preprinted, made herself, or designed by the young lady on a computer if she has access to one.

Your Daughter Is Becoming
a Young Lady If . . .

She handwrites her own thank-you notes.

She acknowledges a gift with a thank-you note as
promptly as possible.

She includes a reference in the thank-you note
referring to the specific gift. She does not say,
"Thank you for the birthday present."

She sends a thank-you note if she has been
someone's guest on a special vacation or outing.

She understands privacy issues when it comes to
mail, via the postal service or the Internet, and
never opens or reads another person's mail.

Parent Pointers

Handwrite your thank-you notes in a timely and
personal fashion.

Occasionally, for no special reason, send letters or
postcards to your child. Everyone loves to get
mail.

Get your daughter in the habit of writing thank-
you notes as young as possible; if she can pick
up a crayon, she is ready.

Allow your daughter to choose a box of her
own stationery and give her a supply of her
own return address labels and stamps. Girls

especially like things they can use—rubber stamps or paper punchers—to decorate their own stationery.

If she is too young to do so, address the envelopes for her as soon as she completes the letters.

Take your daughter to the post office or mailbox to drop her letters.

Try This at Home

In addition to a well-organized system of photo albums and the traditional baby book, my mother kept one large cardboard box for each of her children. In it, she saved all kinds of things: a lock of our baby hair, the first tooth we lost, our first drawings, our report cards, award certificates, baby bracelets, and our first pair of shoes. She also kept all the birthday cards we received from our first birthday until our teens, and then the letters we all wrote home after we had moved out on our own. Every bit of it is precious and priceless, but the cards and letters we received are a wonderful reminder of all the people who have cared about us since even before we were born. The letters we wrote home once we had grown send us hurtling back through the years to our youth, our dreams, and our disappointments. She presented us with our boxes as we each turned thirty; I have been keeping the same for my children and know they will treasure it just as much as I do.

Some Good Advice

E-mail has replaced letter writing; Evites are speedier and cheaper than printed invitations. There are sites that allow you to design greeting cards for every occasion via the Internet. Family portraits and vacation photos are posted on Facebook. In response, the United States Postal Service will be cutting back on delivery days. If UPS and FedEx take over package deliveries, will handwritten correspondence cease to exist? I hope not. How do you save a text that says "I love you Mommy" or a tweet that says "Camp is fun but I miss you Daddy"? Even if you rarely use the US mail, leave your daughter a handwritten note—tucked into her lunch box, on her dresser, in her backpack— every so often. "Congratulations on the great report card, honey!" "Thank you for taking your brother to the park!" "Have fun with Grandma this weekend!" Before my children were readers and writers, I created a sign-off that is part letter, part (very primitive) drawing, that I use to sign every note, every letter, every greeting card I write to them. The first time my daughter signed a card to me the same way, it brought tears to my eyes, and connected us in a way no electronic communication is capable of doing.

Chapter Twenty-two

GIVING AND RECEIVING

Every December since I was seven years old, I have hung the same special ornament on my Christmas tree. It began its holiday decorating career as a red Christmas ball, onto which was glued a pair of blue eyes, a nose, and a bow-shaped mouth; a little felt Santa hat with a piece of holly was perched on top, and from under the hat hung two braids of yellow yarn.

Until I left home, it was stored with all of our other family ornaments, but it was never unwrapped or hung up by anyone but me. When I left at nineteen to move to New York City, along with my clothes, furniture, family photos, books, records, and diaries, I took the ornament, wrapped in tissue paper in a small box. That first lonely Christmas in my tiny studio apartment, it was the only decoration I placed on my tabletop tree. My collection of ornaments has grown larger every year, but it all started with that one little ball that moved with me everywhere I went. Over the years, it cracked from one side to another, and I taped it back up again. Then it lost one eye, then its nose, and finally, the ball itself became so shattered it was not repairable. The only thing that now remains on the hook is the hat and the braids, and they are looking pretty shabby too. A couple of years ago, my children were laughing at the raggedy thing and asked me why I didn't just throw it away. Here is what I told them.

When I was seven years old, my Brownie troop celebrated Christmas by making stockings of personal items and bringing them to a nursing home for senior citizens, where we sang Christmas carols and had punch and cookies. Afterward, we returned to the church where we held our meetings for the eagerly awaited gift exchange. Every Brownie had been told to bring a gift with a three-dollar limit; the wrapped presents were put in a pile, and one by one, we chose one and opened it. I was the last to pick and watched as the other Brownies opened boxes of colored pencils, a game, or small pieces of jewelry. Finally, it was my turn and I opened the last small box. Inside was the ornament. I was sorely disappointed at such a useless gift, and if the look on my face wasn't obvious enough, I saw fit to say aloud, "What *is* this?" with a tone of utter dismay.

As soon as the words left my mouth, I knew I had done something really wrong. The little girl who had contributed the ornament—which she had made with her mother—burst into tears. My ignominy was heightened by the fact that my mother was the Brownie leader. She was astonished at this behavior from her own child, and she snatched me up from my seat so quickly I thought she would pull my arm out of its socket. She marched me out of the room and into the hall, where she told me in no uncertain terms that she had never been so embarrassed or so ashamed of me. Of course I had to apologize to my fellow Brownie, and to her mother when she came to pick up her daughter; for the rest of the year, she didn't speak to me, and I didn't blame her a bit.

When we got home, I was sent to my room, where I flung myself on my bed and cried and cried. Finally, my mother came in and, somewhat calmed down, gave me a lecture on kindness, decency, consideration, and respect, but it wasn't really necessary; the little girl's hurt face that afternoon spoke volumes and had already taught me all I needed to know. I wrote her a thank-you note, with another apology, then hung the ornament on our tree.

For the first several years after that Christmas, every time I hung the ornament I was again overwhelmed with shame and regret at my actions that day. Over time, the sting has lessened, but I have never once hung that ornament without its attendant reminder of my thoughtless action.

I didn't relish sharing that story with my children, but I hope it accomplished a few things. They saw that even their mother, still perfect in every way to a seven- and eight-year-old, had once (if only it *were* just once) done something very wrong. They learned that when we do something wrong, we must make recompense; that receiving graciously is a gift you return to the giver, and that causing someone unnecessary hurt will cause you the far greater pain. My mother had forgotten the entire incident until I brought it up a few years ago; I'll bet that the little girl hasn't given it a thought in years and years. Because of what my parents had already taught me about how to treat others, and thanks to a tiny Santa hat that hangs on a crooked hook, I will never forget that afternoon. As painful as it is, I am grateful for the reminder.

More than anything else, good parents give their children daily examples of respect, kindness, consideration, honor, generosity, empathy, charity, compassion, and grace. These are the most profound gifts you can bestow upon your children, and the ones that will last their lifetime.

ABOUT THE AUTHOR

*K*ay West has been a professional writer in Nashville, TN for 30 years. She was restaurant critic for the *Nashville Scene* for 15 years and remains a contributing feature writer. She is Nashville stringer for *People*. She has written four books, including *How to Raise a Lady* and *How to Raise a Gentleman*, and co-authored *Dani's Story: A Journey From Neglect to Love*. She has raised a well-mannered daughter and a well-mannered son and is an avid baseball fan.

INDEX

written replies to, 185

J

K

L

M